THE BOOK OF
HELSTON

ANCIENT BOROUGH AND MARKET TOWN

REG JENKIN WITH DEREK CARTER

HALSGROVE

First published in Great Britain in 2000,
Revised and reprinted 2012

Copyright © Reg Jenkin and Derek Carter 2012

All rights reserved. No part of this publication may be reproduced,
stored in a retrieval system, or transmitted
in any form or by any means without the prior permission
of the copyright holder.

British Library Cataloguing-in-Publication Data
A CIP record for this title is available from the British Library

ISBN 978 0 85704 184 5

HALSGROVE
Halsgrove House,
Ryelands Business Park,
Bagley Road, Wellington, Somerset TA21 9PZ
Tel: 01823 653777   Fax: 01823 216796
email: sales@halsgrove.com

Part of the Halsgrove group of companies.
Information on all Halsgrove titles is available at: www.halsgrove.com

Printed in China by Everbest Printing Co Ltd

Preface

Since the first publication of *The Book of Helston* in 2000, many changes have taken place in the town. Reg and Derek have decided through public demand to extend the publication into the twenty-first century.

Helston has grown considerably over the last decade. An Henlys, a new estate on the outskirts of the town, has increased the population considerably. A new supermarket and an extension to another, help provide for their needs. The closure of Helston's Community Centre in Penrose Road caused a great deal of distress to many organisations. This fine building was a gift to the people of Helston by the great Victorian benefactor, John Passmore Edwards.

The former Cattle Market on the Lower Green closed in 2001. Now a fine multi-purpose building has been built on the site and aptly named "The Old Cattle Market". This provides a venue for a large Farmers' Market, office accommodation and several rooms for community use. This building, along with the Lakeside Café, Skateboard Park, Children's Playground and "events square" gives a whole new dimension to the area and is enjoyed by young and old alike.

This year sees the centenary of the Coronation Lake and Park, built to commemorate the Coronation of King George V and Queen Mary. Celebrations will be held to mark the occasion and also the Diamond Jubilee of the reign of Queen Elizabeth II, our present monarch.

Helston still retains some of its ancient character and manages to provide a good selection of shops – long may it continue to do so. Perhaps with the help of the newly-appointed Town Manager, Helston will once again be known, as in days gone by, as the "Metropolis of the West".

This new publication will, I'm sure, be as readily accepted as the first.

MARTIN MATTHEWS
CARER HELLYS
FREEMAN OF HELSTON

HELSTON.

Inex Trenerry, hairdresser of Wendron Street and keen motor enthusiast.

A very faded print of Sir Montague Rogers' new car. The photograph was taken outside Thomas' which began as a wheelwright's business and diversified into coach building. Left to right: Norman Williams, ?, ?, James Henry Thomas, Billy Burrows.

Helston and the Lizard Area Celebrates the Queen's Diamond Jubilee

Over the four day period, Saturday 2 June to Tuesday 5 June 2012, the people of Helston and the Lizard Peninsula celebrated the Queen's Diamond Jubilee with a wide range of activities. The weather over the four days was dominated by wind and showers, but despite this Street Parties and picnics took place across the area. From Sithney to Lizard Town the bunting flew, flags were waved and Union Jack hats were in abundance.

Several local schools held their own Jubilee celebration parties before the bank holiday weekend. At Parc Eglos Primary School, in Helston, the whole school enjoyed a special party lunch outside. Tables dressed with Union Jack table cloths were laden with sandwiches, biscuits, crisps and

Mad Hatter's Tea Party in Meneage Street.

Street Party at Parc Eglos.

cakes, while children wore clothes in red, white and blue. Garas School pupils enjoyed a parade around the playground dressed in red, white and blue and wearing their self-made crowns. This they followed with a street/playground tea party and were later presented with a jubilee medal, mug and bookmark. In Porthleven schoolchildren, including the singing choir, sang songs to begin the Jubilee Celebrations. This again was followed by Tea and the presentation of jubilee mugs.

In Helston Town Centre the main event took place on Saturday, with a street market, vintage car display and a giant Mad Hatter's Tea Party along Meneage Street. With rolling grey clouds overhead and the occasional spattering of rain, 200 guests remained in fine form to enjoy a slap up tea. They were joined by a host of colourful characters, including Gary Hunt as a 1940s' tea lady and town centre manager Jonathan Birkett as a clown.

As the rain came in heavier over the course of the afternoon the day's programme of events went ahead almost as planned, with the weather only forcing cancellations from Helston Town Band and the Anchor Morris Men. Still performing were Samba Celtica, Da Levies Dancing, Movin' Toon and Pretty Suite, who played to a peak of between 120 and 150 revellers at one stage.

Mark Upton, from the Epworth Hall committee that organised the day, said: "It was an excellent day. There was really positive feedback." He thanked everybody that helped, as well as the Park Café, Warren's Bakery and Horse & Jockey Bakery for their donations of food and funders Helston Rotary, Helston-Lizard Rotary, Cober Valley Rotary, Cornwall Councillors Judith Haycock,

Samba Celtica lead the parade down Coinagehall Street during Saturday's Festivities in the town.

Andy Wallis and Alec Robertson, and Helston Town Council.

At the same time a Jubilee Family Fun Day took place at Helston Community Field, organised by the Light and Life Church. The day had a "traditional" theme, with old-fashioned games and activities, a craft tent for children and a teddy bears picnic for under fives. On Tuesday 89 adults and 39 children attended a street party in Barton Close, the cul-de-sac being closed for the celebrations.

In the villages across the Peninsula various celebrations took place

Mullion held three days of celebrations, with the main event taking place on Sunday with fancy dress in St Mellan's Park followed by a big jubilee lunch, family entertainment and games. A beacon bonfire was then lit on Monday, as part of a mass lighting around the country.

Coverack held their Jubilee events on Saturday with a sandcastle and sand crown building competition, while in St Keverne on Monday there was a children's decorated crown competition, ox roast and family sports on the playing field. This was followed by a torchlight procession to Trythance, for the lighting of the Jubilee Beacon.

In Ashton the whole community came together on Sunday for a village committee tea party and summer fete behind the Lion & Lamb pub, while in Manaccan there was a fancy dress competition on Monday, followed by games and a street party by the church.

Porthleven and Ruan Minor suffered the worst weather out of all the villages, having planned their events for Tuesday that saw heavy rain for much of the day.

The Porthleven 'Picnic in the Park', planned for The Moors quickly became the 'Picnic in the Public Hall' after organisers made the decision at 9am to move everything indoors. The tug of war and games were postponed and were planned to be held on Lifeboat Day instead, although the Da Levies dance group still managed to put on a colourful display on the stage. Music came from Porthleven School Signing Choir. Despite the change of venue everyone still turned out in full force and the Public Hall was transformed in two hours.

Ruan Minor had planned a range of activities on the recreation ground, ranging from maypole dancing and sideshows to live bands. Pride of place at the event was a four-tier cake made by young Harry Deacon, with children given mugs specially designed by Andre Ellis.

St Martin's main celebrations took place on the Saturday and contained several longer term memorials including the planting of a Jubilee Copper Beech tree, and the opening of a newly constructed footpath for children from the their school to the Parish Hall car-park to avoid walking along a dangerous road through the village. The path was appropriately signed "Diamond Jubilee Path". The presentation of medallions for all the children and the awarding of prizes for the winners of the Fancy Dress Parade, the best dressed house and garden took place in a packed Parish Hall, which was then followed with a scrumptious Jubilee Tea served to 120 people of all ages. Later in the evening, despite the rain, at Newtown in St Martin, games were arranged for the children and a comic football match was enjoyed by all.

On the Monday evening beacons were lit in places including Sithney, Mullion, The Lizard and St Anthony.

They were the Peninsula's contribution to a national chain of beacons, the final one of which was lit at the end of the Jubilee Concert outside Buckingham Palace.

The four children were Junior Road Safety Officers (JRSOs), together with Mrs Nicholls, the oldest former ex St Martin pupil, who cut the tape, and Brindley Hosken who uncovered the path sign.

Some 120 guests enjoying a scrumptious Jubilee Tea, which was a "Faith Tea" organized by members of St Martin Lunch Club.

Contents

Preface — 3
Helston and the Lizard Area Celebrates The Queen's Diamond Jubilee — 5
First Charter of King John 15th April 1201 — 9
Introduction — 11

Chapter 1: Families From Back-Along — 17
- The Jenkins — 17
- Sir Thomas Holland — 19
- The Jameses — 21
- W.J. Winn — 23

Chapter 2: Meneage Street and Around 1880–1930 — 29
- Meneage Street — 30
- Trengrouse Way — 44
- The Workhouse or Union — 45
- Upper Meneage Street — 48
- Furry Way and Whitehill — 53
- Meneage (lizard) Road and Helston Downs — 55

Chapter 3: Helston, the Town of My Youth 1920–39 — 57
- Wendron Street — 57
- St John's Ambulance and Upper Wendron Street — 61
- Penrose Road and Shute Hill — 63
- Godolphin Road — 65
- Station Road — 67
- Turnpike and Clodgey Lane and a Walk Around Coinagehall Street — 72
- Helston Kennels — 74
- Lower Coinagehall Street — 75
- Church Street — 85
- Cross Street — 91
- St John's — 93
- For King and Country — 98

Chapter 4: Life between the Wars 1918–39 — 101
- Helston Roads — 102
- Attending Chapel in Helston — 103
- School Days — 107
- My First Job, Town Time, Saturdays in Helston and Funerals — 109
- Work at the Haberdashers, Slaughterhouses and the Leather Industry — 111

Chapter 5: The War Years 1939–45 — 113
- The Approach of War — 113
- News from Back Home — 116
- Back to Blighty — 117
- Meeting My Future Wife — 119

Chapter 6: Post-War Helston 1945–99 — 121
- Back to Civvy Street — 121
- Material Changes in the Decorating Business — 123
- Helston, An Expanding Town — 125

Chapter 7: Flora Days — 127

Chapter 8: Reggie in Retirement 1980-2000 — 135
- Missing Sisters and the Symons Family — 135
- Exploring the Past and Beating the Bounds — 137
- Helston Valley Tin Company and J. Rapson Champion Coal Carrier — 138

Conclusion — 141
Helston at the Start of the Twenty First Century — 157

Hill's Hotel, c.1920.

Angel Hotel in Coinagehall Street, 1903. (Courtesy Gerald Trethowan)

First Charter of King John
15th April 1201

2001 was a very special year for Helston folk. Friends from all over the world were welcomed to share in the Town's celebration of Helston's eight hundred years since King John granted Helston folk "all the freedoms of a free borough".

On April 14th, on the eve of this eight hundredth anniversary of our receiving a Royal Charter, Helston lit a beacon to begin a season of joyous events – processions, parades, pageants, exhibitions, concerts, rallies and street parties- which ran until December.

Prince Charles also took great pleasure in meeting with Martin Matthews, the Curator of Helston Folk Museum, and the Mayor of Helston, the late Donald Eddy.

John, by the grace of God King of England, Lord of Ireland, Duke of Normandy and Aquitane, Count of Anjou, to the Arch-bishops, Bishops, Abbots, Earls, Barons, Justiciars, Sheriffs, and all Bailiffs, and to his faithful subjects, Greeting.

Know ye that we have granted and by our present charter have confirmed that our borough of Helston be a free borough, and that our burgesses of the same town have a gild merchant, and quittance throughout our whole land from toll, pontage, passage, stallage, lastage, and soilage, saving, in all things, the liberties of the city of London.

We grant also to them that they not be compelled to plead, except within their own borough, of matters or tenements belonging to their town, except in pleas belonging to our Crown, and in pleas concerning lands outside the borough.

We will, also, that they have all the other liberties and free customs which our burgesses of the castle of Launceston had in the time of King Henry our father, with the proviso that none of the aforesaid burgesses, unless he be resident in the aforesaid town of Helston, shall have these liberties.

These are the witnesses: W. Earl of Salisbury, W. Briwer, Robert of Turham, Robert of Tregoz, Simon of Pateshull, Ralph of Stoke, Eustace of Fauconberg.

Given by the hand of Simon, Archdeacon of Wells, at Cranborne, on the 15th day of April in the second year of our reign.

Plaque opened at Meneage House by Prince Charles

During the month of May 2001 HRH The Duke of Cornwall made a special visit to the town and during his time here unveiled commemorative plaques at the Gryll's Monument in Coinagehall Street and at Meneage House.

*The Old Market House, built in 1576. Demolished 1837-38.
The building consisted of the Meat and Corn Market, and at its north end the Guildhall.
The present Guildhall and Corn Exchange stand on part of the site.*

Market Place in 1890.

Top: *Children of Wendron Street.*

Above: *Harry Hawk, butcher of Wendron Street, delivering meat to outlying areas.*

INTRODUCTION

Helston stands on the river Cober, part of which still tumbles down the kennels at the sides of the main streets – as it has done for 200 years. The river, once rich in alluvial tin, provided great wealth to the town which is bounded by Wendron to the north and east, Sithney to the west, and Mawgan and Gunwalloe to the south. It is essentially a four-cross town centred on Market Place with Wendron Street to the east, Meneage Street to the south, Coinagehall Street to the west and Church Street to the north.

Although the town itself is over 1000 years old Helston did not become a separate parish until 1845. It became a borough, however, in 1201, and was a royal manor in about AD930. Undoubtedly it was a tribal capital, which grew up around the castle and had become a place of considerable importance by the time of Edward the Confessor. In 1066 it was held by Harold, Earl of Cornwall, but was passed to William the Conqueror who in turn gave it to his half brother Robert, Count of Mortain. In 1140 the manor passed to the illegitimate son of Henry I, Reginald de Dunstanville, but reverted to the Crown when he died on 1 July 1175. On Henry II's death in 1189, the earldom and manor passed to John, but it again reverted to the Crown when John rebelled against his brother, King Richard I.

In feudal times the lord of the manor held absolute sway over the lives of the serfs and villeins who, to escape this tyrannical grip, had to become free men, either by purchase or by negotiation. This being accomplished, they then had to obtain a charter conferring rights and privileges. It was in 1201 that the men of Helston petitioned King John that they might have a free town and a 'gild', and gave 40 marks and a light horse for this purpose. The result was the first of Helston's many charters, given on 15 April 1201. Burgesses were compelled to serve as Town Clerk, Tax Collector or Bailiff, whether they wished to accept office or not. This may have played into the hands of those desiring personal power, but it certainly established, through the ages, a tradition of service to the community of which Helston, along with other boroughs, may well be proud.

The author Spencer Toy gives three lists of reeves or mayors for the town: the first from 1284 to 1581; the second an incomplete list from 1585 to 1718; and the third a complete list from 1714 until 1935 (and included at the end of this volume is a further list which brings the names up to the present day). Helston is very fortunate in having a fine collection of mayoral insignia. On formal occasions the Mayor of Helston wears a robe of scarlet cloth edged with sable, and a gold chain equal in value to those of many much larger towns. The robe was purchased by private subscription in 1873, and the chain in a similar way in 1894. The chain at that time cost £263 – at today's prices something in the region of £250,000. It consists of a badge, large centre link, a centre festoon link, and a series of 40 shields with ornamental connections. These shields form a chain of considerable length and are festooned in two rows. On the front face of each shield are elaborate monograms relating to the donors, whilst on the rear faces are inscriptions.

Helston policeman, PC Barber, c.1900.

In 1208 John Wac was appointed Vicar of Wendron and the Chapel of Helston. The borough contained no 'mother' church and was part of the ecclesiastical parish of Wendron, St Michael's Chapel being under the control of the Vicar of Wendron. However, the burgesses had their own Free Chapel of Our Lady, over which the Vicar of Wendron had no control. It was supported by the Cordwainer's Gild and was very well endowed. The chapel stood in the centre of Coinagehall Street, then called Lady Street, and was suppressed in 1547 during the Reformation. Later it was converted into the Coinage Hall. (The present Lady Street was formerly Pig Street, but was renamed by the inhabitants when Coinagehall Street gave up its former title.).

Helston received another charter from King John, and by 1225 the earldom had been conferred on Richard, John's second son and brother of King Henry III. By the time that the town had received two further charters from this prince it was clearly an important tin centre and market town. In 1265 King Henry III commended the burgesses of Helston to the citizens of Bordeaux and Rochelle when they came to their ports bearing cargos of tin.

Helston returned two members to Parliament from 1298 until the Reform Bill of 1832, when the number was reduced to one. The borough lost its representation in 1885 under the Redistribution of Seats Act. The list of members bears many famous Cornish names, including Godolphin, Vyvyan, Killigrew, Carew, Penrose, Rogers and Antron. The last member for the borough was Walter Molesworth St Aubyn.

The suburb of St Johns is named after the Priory and Hospital of St John, which stood for upwards of 300 years from 1260 near the bridge over the Cober, and was probably used by pilgrims travelling to and from St Michael's Mount. A stone coffin lid, found in a hedge at St Johns in 1918, is now in the north aisle of Sithney Church and is probably the only relic of the Priory.

The Church of St Michael, in the charge of the Vicar of Wendron, stood at the north end of the town and its 90-foot spire was visible from the sea. The church, badly damaged by storm in 1727, was in ruins by 1753, when a decision was made to rebuild it; after many delays the new church was opened on 18 October 1761. The funds necessary for the building were given entirely by Lord Godolphin, as is commemorated on a chandelier which hangs in the church. It has a modern East window, which incorporates the music of the Furry Dance. The tower, 103 feet high, has a fine peal of eight bells. The registers date from 1598 and some fine silver-gilt church plate from 1630; a modern silver chalice and paten is dated 1928. In the porch are ancient brasses dedicated to the Bougins family which came from the old church.

On 5 April 1548 the town was the scene of a dramatic religious riot. William Body was appointed by the commissioners to remove all shrines, tables, candlesticks, paintings, pictures and monuments from churches and chapels, in accordance with the provisions of the Chantries Act. He paid for this action with his life, being murdered in a house in Church Street. The rioters, drawn from many surrounding parishes, were led by Martin Geoffry, Vicar of St Keverne, and by William and John Kilter of Constantine. Several rioters were arrested, tried and condemned for murder and for treason, and were hung, drawn and quartered. This local riot was followed by the more serious Cornish Prayer Book Rebellion at Bodmin in 1549.

Other religious disturbances took place in 1753 when John Wesley first preached in Helston. *The Diocesan History* states that Wesley was the victim of savage attacks at Helston, opposition to him being more active and determined in West Cornwall than in other parts of the country. Things improved, however, as recorded in his journal for 10 September 1765:

... preached at St Johns near Helston, once as furious a town as Redruth, now almost all the gentry of the town were present and heard with the deepest attention.

It was on this occasion that Wesley preached in the first dissenting chapel in Helston, built near the bridge at St Johns in around 1760. A new chapel, Epworth Hall, built early in the 19th century, was replaced by the present building in 1888.

Helston had a grammar school in the 16th century, but the name of its founder and the date of its foundation are unknown. Records reveal that the school was rebuilt in 1610, replaced by a new building at the end of the 1600s, and again rebuilt in 1834. The Revd Derwent Coleridge was headmaster from 1827 to 1841, when the school enjoyed a considerable reputation. Just 20 years later, however, the institution declined and was closed not long afterwards. The County Secondary School was built in 1905 and a fine new Helston County School building was opened at Gwealhellis on 6 February 1939.

Although Helston was a coinage town in 1305, tin was not coined here until about 200 years later. By then, tinning had become increasingly prosperous and by the 1800s the industry was at its height, with nearly 100 mines being worked in the area. On Wheal Voar pay day Sithney Hill would be crowded with miners on their way to Helston to spend their money, and there were many fierce clashes between the Breage miners and those of Sithney and Wendron in and around the many public houses of the town.

A prominent feature of the town is the monument to Humphrey Millett Grylls, member of a well-known Cornish family, a Freeman and four times Mayor of Helston. A banker, he rendered great service to the community during a depression in mining, and his death in April 1834, at the early age of 45, was felt as a great loss. Over 2000 persons contributed towards his memorial, the foundation stone of which was laid on 23 October 1834.

Another, far less showy, monument stands outside the south door of the Parish Church and is dedicated to Henry Trengrouse, who died on 19 February 1854. He devoted over 40 years of his life and most of his fortune to the invention and adaption of the rocket apparatus. Born at Mullion on 18 March 1772 and educated at Helston Grammar School, he began his working life as a cabinet maker. The wreck of HMS *Anson* on the Loe Bar on 29 December 1807 brought with it the

INTRODUCTION

tragic loss of over 100 lives and made a profound impression on Trengrouse. In 1791, Lt John Ball suggested that for the rescue of those shipwrecked a shot with a chain attached should be fired from a mortar to the ship. This idea was developed by Captain Mamby, but was found to be dangerous to life. Trengrouse, after seeing a firework display at Helston during George III's birthday celebrations, conceived the idea of fixing a line to a rocket and the first experimental firework was launched at Porthleven in 1816. Many journeys were made to and from London and on 25 February 1818 the apparatus was exhibited before the Admiralty, who reported on it favourably. The Government, after ordering 20 sets, decided to make the apparatus and paid Trengrouse £50 for estimated loss of profit. He continued to fight bitter opposition and as late as 23 December 1828 wrote a letter to the *Sailors' Magazine* signed 'Samaritanus', urging all 'professed friends of sailors to do everything possible to prevent loss of life through shipwreck'. Apart from receiving a diamond ring from the Czar of Russia in recognition of his invention, Trengrouse was practically without honour in his own generation. Although little was done for one who achieved so much, the self-sacrifice and persistence against prejudice and opposition of this noble and unselfish man has now been fully recognised.

Those who drowned at the wreck of the *Anson* were buried, according to existing custom, on the cliff-top, and without shroud, coffin or burial service. Public conscience was so aroused that Thomas Grylls of Helston formed a bill which was presented to Parliament and then by the Grylls Act of 1808 which provided that:

> *... the bodies of all persons washed ashore should be laid to rest with Christian rites in the nearest churchyard at the expense of the parish.*

Mr Tobias Roberts of Helston who, with Mr Foxwell of Mullion, received the Humane Society's silver medal for rescue operations at the *Anson* wreck, projected a scheme for a harbour refuge at Porthleven for the many ships seeking shelter at Mount's Bay in time of storm. The advantages of a harbour at the Loe Pool and at Porthleven were considered, preference was given to the latter, an Act of Parliament obtained in 1811 and operations commenced thereafter. Although the harbour failed to provide the desired haven because of the difficulty of entry in rough weather, it proved of great commercial value.

In 1837 plans for turning the Loe Pool into a harbour, with a canal which would allow vessels of up to 300 tons to come up to Helston, were considered but not adopted. This was perhaps fortunate, as the development would have ruined the beauty of a spot which should always remain in its natural state.

There is strong evidence that the Cober was a tidal river probably long before the 10th century, and the castle overlooking the Cober Valley was possibly a defence for the town against marauders sailing up the estuary before the entrance was blocked. Helston had jurisdiction over the port of Gweek before the 14th century – a right, it is said, which they acquired when they lost their own port. Mount's Bay is a place of strong currents, and even within living memory there have been vast quantities of shingle frequently shifted from Porthleven to Gunwalloe, as well as in the reverse direction, with a build-up at the Loe Bar. From time to time tidal waves have also been observed to completely alter the formation of the beach. The Bar is open to the full force of south-westerly gales, and those who have seen the magnificent and awe-inspiring sight of huge seas breaking over the Bar into the Loe Pool and the flooding of the Cober Valley up to Helston will not find it hard to believe that Helston was once open to the sea. Before the construction of an adit, the rising Loe occasionally flooded the lower reaches of the town and in the winter of 1822 it was possible for Captain F. Rogers, R.N., of Penrose, to sail his yacht right up to the town, where he fired his guns in salute. To relieve flooding, Helston's mayor used to send a purse containing three halfpence to the lord of the manor with a request for permission to cut the Bar (a custom so old that its origin cannot be traced). Permission being given, a trench was dug in the shingle and the waters of the lake rushed into the sea, causing much commotion over a great distance, with discolouration even as far away as the Scilly Isles.

In Helston 8 May is the traditional day upon which Flora Day, with its Furry Dance and Hal-an-Tow ceremony, is held. The dance, evidently a survivor of paganism, was appropriated by the early church as a festival connected with St Michael, the patron saint of the town. The character of the dance has been carefully preserved through the centuries and it remains a dignified, yet delightful and happy, ceremony. Great wisdom was shown by the stewards when, in 1922, they introduced a children's dance at 10.15a.m. (considered by many to be the

Lt Col G.J. Fletcher, 6th Bn DCLI, taking over the 1st Bn Colours from the 1st Bn Cadre Colour Party.
Insets: EH101 Merlin and the sign outside the perimeter fence of Culdrose.

INTRODUCTION

best of the day), thereby handing on the tradition to the younger generation. The Hal-an-Tow ceremony, which had fallen by the wayside by the 19th century, was revived by the Helston Old Cornwall Society in 1930 and is now firmly re-established. Once again, the children of the town were involved, with the co-operation of headmasters and teachers who trained pupils in singing the song and carrying out the ceremony which forms probably the oldest part of the day's proceedings.

Helston has a very fine Folk Museum, established in 1949 after much pioneering work by the local Old Cornwall Society. It has sections devoted to domestic life, agriculture, archaeology, mining and transport, with implements, tools, coins, clothing, pictures and photos of local interest on display. In 1999 it was extended to include the old Drill Hall and it is a museum which should be seen by every lover of Cornwall.

The ancient borough of Helston was modernised on 1 April 1934, when the boundaries were extended to include parts of the parishes of Wendron and Sithney, the latter including Porthleven – at one time a busy fishing port with a large fleet of vessels, not only in Mount's Bay and around the Cornish and Devon coasts, but as far away as Scotland and Ireland. This industry has, unfortunately, declined, together with the boat-building industry, which at one time employed over 200 men.

The harbour, the most south-westerly in Britain, was once a busy place, witness to imports of coal, cement, lime and manures, and exports of tin, china clay and granite. Decline in these fundamental interests, coupled with the development of alternative means of transport, affected the growth of the port although there is still an important net-manufacturing industry.

Porthleven became a separate ecclesiastical parish from Sithney in 1845 and the Church of St Bartholomew, built shortly afterwards, was the gift of the Rogers family, whose ancestor purchased the Manor of Penrose in the year 1770. A Methodist chapel has been in use here since 1840.

In the years following the Second World War Helston once again experienced a period of rapid expansion, in the main due to the building of RNAS Culdrose. Its population in 1946 was 4950 and in 1998 stands at 9355.

Ready for flight from Eglos Dairy Fields, Helston Downs, 1924.

The Jenkin Family

Clockwise from above: *Grandma Jenkin (née Oppy) and Rosenia (born 1850) as a child; Aunt Rosenia Jenkin, who sailed around Cape Horn at the age of 5 and spent her childhood in Bolivia living in a mining village where her father worked in the copper mines; the twin Jenkin sisters, Reggie's Aunt Catherine (Katie) and Aunt Phillipa (Tilly); Catherine at a later date as midwife with John Woods of 50 Meneage Street; Reggie's father, S.H. Jenkin as a young man.*

Chapter 1: Families From Back-Along

GRANDFATHER BENJAMIN JENKIN

I always believed that my father came from a Helston family, but in actual fact he did not. Grandfather Benjamin was a St Day man and was born there on 22 February 1819. He became a sawyer and was much involved in mining, cutting pit props and the like. On Christmas Day 1841 he married Eliza Oppy and whilst living and working in St Day and Redruth they had five children: Benjamin Richard (1845), John (1846), Eliza Jane (1849), Rosenia (1850) and William (1852). By this time the copper mines were in decline and Cornish miners were being offered the opportunity to go to the copper fields in Bolivia. By signing a six-year contract whole families were given living accommodation and free return passage to Bolivia.

Benjamin took the bold option of signing such a contract and in March 1855 left St Day for Portreath with his wife Eliza and their five young children to catch a sailing boat for Swansea, which was by then the centre for copper smelting and from where ore-carrying boats sailed regularly to and from Bolivia and Chile. The departure date was unfixed so the family stayed in a Swansea boarding house until the boat was ready to leave.

It was a three-month voyage which took the family right across the Atlantic, down around Cape Horn and up the other side to northern Chile from where they travelled into land-locked Bolivia. Tragically, little Eliza Jane died before the end of her father's six-year contract, although another child, Emily, was born there in 1860. In about 1862 the family returned to Cornwall and lived in Blight's Row in Redruth. There the birth of my father, Samuel Robert Jenkin, on 12 June 1866, followed that of his twin sisters Phillipa and Catherine. The other three boys who came back from Bolivia with Grandfather went mining at Poldice, St Day. When they came of age, in their late teens, Grandpa Benjamin again took them back to Chile and left his wife and younger members of the family at home in Cornwall. For the 1871 census all of the men were away, and the family living at Roskrows Road, Redruth, was listed as including: Eliza Jane (47); Rosenia (20, a milliner); Emily (11); Phillipa and Catherine (8 – twins born at Redruth); Samuel Robert (4 – also born at Redruth). Grandfather left all three boys in Chile but came back himself and opened up a boot and shoe shop at the bottom of the High Street in Redruth. He opened another shop in St Agnes and then he came to Helston and opened a third shop where Lloyds Bank is now. It was there (*left*) that the family lived in a flat over the shop.

Meneage Street before the bank was built. Benjamin Jenkin lived in the upper storey of the building on the left of the picture with his wife and children. The building closest to the camera was the new Post Office, originally the Duke's Head. The corner shop was Reed & Roberts the drapers.

Benjamin himself went on the road selling boots and shoes. In those days there were boot and shoe makers almost everywhere and he used to buy his wares and take them by pony and trap to Redruth, calling in at mines on the way and selling them to the miners, before picking up another lot at Redruth. From here he would go to St Agnes, again selling at the mines and farms en-route before returning to Redruth where he would stay the night, pick up another load and re-sell on the return journey to Helston. Grandpa Benjamin died in 1888 at Wendron Street, Helston, aged 69, leaving Eliza to outlive him by a decade. She died in Camborne aged 76.

Of my three uncles who went to Chile only one, Benjamin Richard, returned. He became a mine agent in South America and came back to Helston to die later in Bodmin at the age of 48. John married a local lady, changed his name to Juan, remained in Chile and adopted the Catholic faith. William married in Chile but went to Australia.

Back in Cornwall my Aunt Phillipa, known as Tilly, was working in her father's boot and shoe business in the early 1880s and by 1888 was living in Market Street, Penryn, where she was perhaps managing yet another similar store. After her father died she married Frank Cornelius. They kept a greengrocers business in the Strand, Dawlish, had five children and were often visited by her sister Rosenia who was by then living in Teignmouth.

Father Samuel Jenkin

Reggie's father, 1895.

Father (*left*) went to Mr Gill's private school behind the church. Among the many pupils with him there were Tommy Holland, who later became Sir Thomas Holland, and a boy with the same surname as himself (although of no relation), William Jenkin, who became 'Old Mr Jenkin' at St Anthony. When father left school he became an apprentice blacksmith at Holmans of Camborne. On Monday mornings he used to walk from Helston to Camborne and returned again on Saturday afternoons. During the week he lodged at Penponds with his sister Auntie Katie Dale, a nurse. Auntie Katie had emigrated with her husband and young family to South Australia, but unfortunately her husband died as a young man; his father, Mr Dale of Barton Wendron, then paid for the family's return journey back to Cornwall where he settled them in the house at Penponds. Katie had one daughter, Mary, and three sons who all emigrated to California on the same day! They all did well in America and made regular visits back to Cornwall to see the family.

One evening I was down at St Anthony with my own family and during my visit I had a chat with Old Mr Jenkin. He soon realised who I was:

So you're Harry's son. I've got something to tell you. I was at school with your father and we were good friends. I well remember when he ran away, his parents didn't know where he had gone, but I knew; he told me... but he never told anybody else. I was the only one who knew where he went and I was sworn to secrecy. He was 19 at the time and was living with his parents over where Lloyd's Bank is now. He put his age on to 21 years, used the name Henry, went to Devonport and joined the Navy.

It was the first time that I had heard this story but I was able to confirm it when I examined my father's naval papers. It was perhaps something which he did to escape going down the mines and ending up in Chile like the rest of the boys, but I cannot be sure, as he never spoke about it. Although unknown to me until recently, the story of his naval years and first marriage is a fascinating if tragic story:

Samuel 'Henry' Jenkin, official number 137,398, entered the Navy at Devonport on 4 May 1886, giving his date of birth as 12 June 1864 (although it was actually 11 June 1866). He first saw service as a member of several different gun crews on a wide variety of ships. He rose from armourer's crew in 1886 to Chief Armourer in 1904. In 1893 he married a girl from Helston called Mary Jane Symons whose parents used to keep the shoemaker's shop at 77 Meneage Street just across the road from the Jenkin family (where Halls the chemists is now). 'Henry' and Mary's first child, Erna, was born on 17 March 1894 when Henry was Armourer's Mate on the cruiser *Colossus*. By December he had been promoted to Armourer and the second daughter, Lily, was born on 1 October 1895 when he was serving on the cruiser *Endymion*. Next came Mary, born on 18 December 1898.

Mary Jane was left without a husband for much of the time and had little in the way of family to help her; her elder brother, Humphrey Symons, had emigrated to Kimberley, South Africa, in 1886 (where he was a carpenter – he died in Pietermaritzburg), and her younger brother emigrated to Harrismith in 1894. Tragically Mary Jane died of cancer on 14 June 1907 whilst Harry was serving on the battleship *Vengeance*. He was discharged on 31 May 1908, but was retained on the reserve. His three daughters were by then living with their grandparents at 77 Meneage Street, but in 1909 were moved to live with an aunt in St Austell (see also page 141).

COMMERCIAL & MIDDLE CLASS SCHOOL, Helston.
Principal:—Mr. A. BUTTIMORE.

Mr. JOHN GILL, F.C.S., who carried on the above School for a period of over twenty years has transferred his interests to Mr. Buttimore, who, from his long, varied, and successful experience in teaching, and also in preparing pupils for the Competitive Examinations, feels confidence in his ability to give entire satisfaction to those who may honour him with their support.

The School is now carried on the Second Floor of the Savings' Bank, Church Street, where Mr Buttimore can be consulted.

Pupils prepared for all the Public Examinations and are received between the Terms, viz:—Easter Mid-summer and Michaelmas. TERMS ON APPLICATION

SIR THOMAS HOLLAND

In the 1881 census one Mr John Holland was described as 'a Miller and Farmer of 20 acres, employing two millers and two labourers'. The mill which he operated was at the bottom of Sithney Common Hill, on the outskirts of town, and here he milled oak bark to extract tannin for the treatment of hides at the Cunnack and other tanneries. The Hollands also kept a general stores. At the time of the census the family included the two parents, two daughters (19 and 17) and six sons (15, 13, 11, 9, 7 and 5). The 11-year-old, Thomas, had been recognised as a pupil with great potential and he displayed a keen interest in nature and geology. When the family emigrated to California, Thomas remained behind and lived with the family of Thomas Winkworth, a Helston draper in Coinagehall Street (Simpson's Outfitters).

Thomas started his schooling at the Wesley Day School in Wendron Street, where Mr Winkworth, who was a governor, took a particular interest in him. Later he was transferred to John Gill's Church Hill School, from which, at the age of 16, he gained a National Scholarship entitling him to tuition at the School of Science and Royal School of Mines (now the Imperial College of Science and Technology in Kensington, London). It was here that Thomas came under the influence of T.H. Huxley, who at the time was the College Dean. Four years later, whilst still only 20, the ambitious young Cornishman was admitted as an associate first class.

In 1890, after a short spell as Berkeley Fellow at Owens' College, Manchester, Tom Holland joined the Indian Service and became Assistant Superintendent with the Geological Survey of India, of which, in 1903, he was appointed Director. In this post he was able to employ his talents to the full for the advancement of knowledge in Indian geology and his researches into mineralogy and petrology. He was elected a Fellow of the Royal Society, knighted, and accorded the title of Knight Commander of the Indian Empire.

Retiring from his directorial position in 1909, Sir Thomas became Chairman of the Geological Institute of Manchester. During the First World War he returned to India and in 1916 was appointed President of the Indian Board of Munitions.

Directly after the war he became a member of the Viceroy's Exqutive Committee under Lord Reading, but after three years resigned following a difference of opinion between himself and his senior. Nevertheless, on Thomas' resignation, Lord Reading paid high tribute to his abilities and the work he had done for the benefit of India and Asia.

Professor Michael Swan presenting Mr William Henry Scott, Mayor of Helston, with a framed portrait of Sir Thomas Holland.

On his return to England, Sir Thomas was appointed Rector of the then Imperial College of Science which he had entered so many years before as a very poor, but ambitious, knowledgeable student. From this point on his career was punctuated by a succession of important, and often academic, appointments which led, in 1929, to the post of Principal and Vice-Chancellor of Edinburgh University – a position which he held with dignity and widespread approbation until his final retirement in 1944. As well as the honours bestowed on him for his services in India (K.C.I.E., K.C.S.I.), Sir Thomas Holland earned himself no less than nine honorary degrees.

Such accolades, however, seemed to make little impact on his naturally humble and gracious nature and he never forgot his roots. I well remember a visit he made to our house in the mid-1920s. My father used to go out and sit on the front doorstep of the house and smoke a pipe. One day Sir Thomas came up to him and said: 'Hello you're Jenkin aren't you?... You were Robert Jenkin when we were at school together'. My father looked at him 'some hard' but, failing to recognise him, had to ask him his name. After duly introducing himself as 'Tommy Holland' he joined his old school friend inside for a lengthy discussion of bygone days.

In 1971 Professor Michael Swann, Principal and Vice-Chancellor of Edinburgh University, presented the Mayor of Helston with a framed painting of Sir Thomas by Stanley Cursiter, which now hangs in the Guildhall, providing a visual reminder of this famous Helstonian.

JAMESES AND JENKINS

Above: *Grand-Pa James in the doorway of Trounsons, Church Street.*

Above right: *Uncle Fred (Reggie's mother's second brother) with his grandchildren Susanne and Nigel. A keen supporter of Helston Wesleyan Church, Fred was a builder and lived in Godolphin Road.*

Right: *Three Jenkin boys. John is at the back, Reggie is front left and Percy is front right.*

Left: *The Jameses and Jenkins, 1925. Included are: Catherine James, Harry Jenkin, Mrs Walters (friend of the family), William James, Laura and Percy Jenkin, Phyllis Walters, Erna, John and Reggie Jenkin and Cecilia and Mary Walters.*

FAMILIES FROM BACK-ALONG

THE JAMES FAMILY

My Mother, Laura Lander James, was born on 20 October 1880. Like the rest of her family (except the eldest, Ernie, who was born in Alms House Hill – now Nettle's Hill), she began life in Wendron Street in the old thatched cottage. There were 11 of them born there, and six of them died there before the family moved to 78 Meneage Street, next door to the Union building which has now been converted into housing units.

My mother's father, John James, came from Madron. Penzance was then part of Madron Parish, and in fact he was born in what we now call Penzance near the present-day hospital. He came to Helston and worked at Trounsons in Church Street as a tallow chandler making candles. He was always a most dignified man. On Sundays he wore a top hat and a long-tailed black coat and he was very much engaged in the activities of the Wesleyan chapel in Coinagehall Street. He was a member of the choir for many years before becoming a steward. As a child, I was taken down to the chapel on Sunday mornings by my grandfather. We always sat in the back seat on the left hand side. When the time came to pick up the collection, he would get up, wearing his frocktail coat, and I would catch hold of the tail and walk around behind him. In those days everything was done as a whisper. Miss Ethel Hill who was a very devoted Wesleyan tried to stop me from doing it and to make me sit down on the end of her seat, but I would have none of it and kept hold of Grandpa's tail until he had finished taking up the collection.

Uncle Ernie (*left*), born in 1869, was the eldest and a carpenter, Uncle Fred (born 1871) married Sarah Dally and was a builder, and Uncle William Ewart (born 1890) served his time as a tailor with the Thomases before moving to London where he married Cecilia Taylor. Aunt Katie (born 1875) lived with Aunt and Uncle Richard Tavener because the family house was full and they themselves had no children. Later she married a ship's Captain, James Ellery, and lived at Perranporth. Uncle John Henry (born 1882) was a postman in Helston and married Lilian Grey.

James/Jenkin Family Tree

John James m Alice Ann (Catherine) Lander (see bottom)
(1845–1925)   (1845–1930)

Ernest	Frederick	Kate	John Henry	William Ewart	**Laura Lander**
(1869–1948)	(1871–1950)	(1875–1953)	(1882–1953)	(1890–1946)	**(1880–1969)**
m	m	m	m	m	**m**
Laura Ninnis	Sarah Dally	James Ellery	Lilian Grey	Cecilia Taylor	**Samuel Henry**

Benjamin Jenkin m Elizabeth Oppy
(b.1819)

Samuel Henry	Catherine	Phillipa	Emily	William	Rosenia	Eliz. Jane	John	Benjamin
(1866–1945)	(b.1863)	(b.1883)	(b.1860)	(b.1852)	(b.1850)	(b.1849)	(b.1846)	(1844–92)
m								
Laura Lander								

Samuel Henry Jenkin m **Laura Lander**
(1866–1945)   (1880–1969)

Harry	John	Reg	Percy
(1912–18)	(b.1915)	(b.1916)	(b.1918)

Catherine Lander (1845–1930) had four sisters, three of whom are known:

Elizabeth Ann	Eliza	Emily
m	m	m (1)
Dick Tavener	Mr Kempthorne	Stephen Vincent
		|
		Private John Vincent (Boer War veteran)

Uncle Ernie's wife, Laura Ninnis of Redruth, had an uncle called the Reverend Ninnis who went to China as a missionary. When he returned he brought with him a plate which he gave to my mother. She later passed it on to Percy who has now passed it on to me. Uncle Ernie had one son, Bert, who played the organ at the Baptist chapel and the piano at the cinema and who also had his own dance band. He married twice but had no children and is thought to have gone to work in Bristol during the war. His second wife was called Nellie and they lived at Marazion where they both died.

My maternal grandfather, John James, married Alice Ann Lander (always known as Catherine, *right*). Her father, Richard Lander, born in Helston in 1815, was a boot and shoe maker, with a shop at 77 Meneage Street in the same place as the Symons family. I can remember Mrs Head, who used to have a grocery store there, and when I looked through the census of 1891, she was listed as living with one John Lander, her blind father. My mother and Mrs Head were first cousins, but they never called each other anything but Mrs Head and Mrs Jenkin. Further up the road was Mrs Richards who had another little shop. She was also a cousin to my mother and they too always called each other by their surnames.

Catherine Lander had four sisters. One of them, Elizabeth Ann, married a man named Dick Tavener who worked building railways and came to Helston in the early 1880s when they built the Gwinear Road-Helston section. Another sister, Eliza, married Mr Kempthorne, a soldier who died in Barbados. Eliza lived in Helston for a time and then moved to Gunnislake where she is buried. A third sister, Emily (Aunt Emily Vincent), married Stephen Vincent and lived at 80 Meneage Street, next door to the Poor Law Institution.

Aunt Emily Vincent had a son who went to South Africa to fight in the Boer War. The following is an account from the *West Briton*:

One of the heroes of the Ladysmith siege was Private Johnnie Vincent, 1st Special Ammunition Column. His widowed mother of this town received a letter from him dated March 4th, per last Saturday's Mail. In it he tells a few of his experiences which will never be effaced from his memory. From 30th October until February 27th they were 'shut in' nearly starving on daily rations of – 4 oz biscuit, 4 oz crushed Indian meal, some horse meat (often stinking). No wonder he wasted to the tune of 36lbs; fever and dysentry raged, carrying off an average of ten men a day. There was no medicine and no binding food, and those sent to hospital lay down to die. Most of the time the Boers fired on the hospitals. They lived in holes cut in the hills and behind rocks with plenty of rain to 'wash you out'. Every day there was firing, fighting and starvation; no tobacco and no matches. Articles of consumption were at fabulous prices, and we had no money. The highest prices reached during the siege were 1 dozen matches 13s.6d.; 1 packet of old cigarettes 25s.6d.; 4 ozs cake tobacco 43s.; small chickens 18s.6d.; fresh eggs 48s. a dozen, condensed milk 10s. a tin. By January, flour, sugar, wines and spirits were unobtainable. [One note home read] *'I have had no letter from you since I left England. We expect to go further up country shortly, but they will have to feed us up a bit first. Remember me to all at home.'*

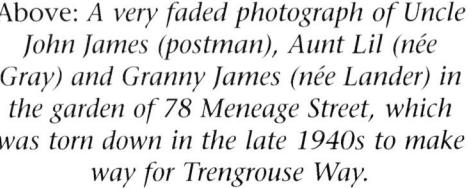

Above: *A very faded photograph of Uncle John James (postman), Aunt Lil (née Gray) and Granny James (née Lander) in the garden of 78 Meneage Street, which was torn down in the late 1940s to make way for Trengrouse Way.*

When this brave hero came back from Ladysmith all of the people in the town got together and presented him with a clock and two side pieces which my mother (his first cousin) later kept on her mantlepiece for many years. When she died, Erna continued to live in the family home at 68 Meneage Street, but eventually moved into the home at Penhellis and the clock was sold. The two side pieces are now in my care.

The cottage where John Jenkin was born up the opening in Meneage Street next to Pascoe's cycle shop.

The Winn Family, c.1903.
Left to right, back: Fred, William H., Ernie; centre: William J. and Mary; front: May, Chrissie, Edith.

Mr W. J. Winn

Mr William John Winn of 72 Godolphin Road was a well-known resident of Helston. Born in the town in 1848 he followed his father's profession of builder and contractor and the Coinagehall Street Methodist Church, Lloyds Bank, Mullion Cove Hotel and Cury Chapel are among the most prominent of his constructions. Several masons and carpenters of later generations, including two of my uncles, served their time with Mr Winn. From a young age he was very active publicly in Helston. He was for many years a member of the Town Council and sat as an alderman. On the death of Mr J. Odger Eva in 1890, Mr Winn was appointed Borough Surveyor, and was mainly responsible for the reconstruction of the cattle market. He was also responsible for the laying out of the Memorial Park and Lake in the lower green which was transformed from a piece of waste land into one of the town's chief attractions. Mr Winn had a life-long association with Church Street United Methodist Church, and for over 60 years was a local preacher on the Helston-Porthleven circuit. He was a long-standing member of the Church Street Choir and the Borough Choral Society, and his services as a soloist were in great demand.

His knowledge of Helston's ancient history was quite astounding and he contributed many articles to the press. In later years he was a prominent member of Helston Old Cornwall Society, enjoyed a long membership of the Helston cricket team, and was instrumental in the formation of Helston Public Institution and Reading Rooms. He also became an active member of Helston Bowling Club and was one of the oldest members of the 'True and Faithful' Lodge of Freemasons, No. 318, Helston.

In 1928 Mr and Mrs Winn celebrated their golden wedding. Mr Winn had a striking and genial personality, which won him a wide circle of friends. He had three sons, William H. of London, Ernest H. of Helston and Frederick J. of Leeds. He also had three daughters, Edith, who kept a high-class millinery shop in Meneage Street, May, a teacher at Wendron Street Methodist School, and Chrissie, a sister in the Royal Free Hospital, London.

A meeting of the Winn and Trengrouse families, with friends, taken at Trevenen House, Meneage Road. The purpose of the gathering remains unknown.

*The Winn family, April 1928.
The picture includes Fred, Ernie, William H., William J., May, Chrissie and Edith.*

Coinagehall Street on Market Day. (Courtesy Gerald Trethowan)

In the late 1920s and early '30s Mr Winn wrote a series of articles which were published in the *West Briton* featuring his memories of Helston. The following is an example:

In my boyhood days, Helston was, as now, 10 miles from everywhere, but with this difference. Now rail and motor bus services enable us to journey comfortably, and speedily, to regions remote and near. Then the travelling facilities were very meagre and poor at the best. Great use was made of vans, four-wheeled conveyances pulled by a single horse [above]. The vans were fitted with plain, boarded seats, and covered with painted canvas for roof and sides, and curtains... to close the front and back. These were laced together to exclude the rain and wind, but often they were far from successful as regards the latter. When the van was crowded this was rather an advantage in the way of ventilation.

Two of these vans gave communication between Helston and Truro. One from Helston to Truro was fortnightly, owned and driven by William Boaden, and the other from Truro to Helston was owned and driven by Richard Cliff. The journey of 17 miles took five to six hours, and if heavily laden a little more than that. Neither of these men was a Band of Hope member, and they frequently arrived at the end of the journey more merry than wise. How could it be otherwise? Between these two towns there were about half a score of public houses, which not only catered for the thirsty but also were depots for receiving parcels and baskets, etc. The drivers on depositing these took a pint 'for the good of the house'. Dobbin was generally very tired before half the journey was over, and always stopped at Rame Cross Halfway House and at the Norway for his horse bag and pail of water. Both driver and passengers often sympathized with Dobbin's hunger and thirst (especially the latter) – so much so that at times the driver experienced difficulty in getting them back to the van to resume the journey.

Lizard was served by William Jose, Hayle by Johno Thomas, on Saturdays only, as also was St Keverne by Tripconey, Constantine (via Gweek) by Medlin, Manaccan by R. James and Porthallow by Jan Mildren. Between Helston and Penzance and Helston and Falmouth there were daily omnibus services, better in every respect than the others described. Also there was a van which went daily to Redruth via Camborne.

In reality Helston was in a state of semi-isolation, and to a large extent found within itself and its immediate surroundings all that its common life required; for example, at one time about 50 families were supported by boot and shoe making. All the boots that were made were of leather from hides supplied by Helston butchers which had been tanned and dressed in the local tanneries, using tannin from oak bark which had been ground at the local mill in St Johns. The clothes that people wore were all made locally. In those days there was no unemployment, though boys began the business life at nine or ten.

The staff of W.J. Winn, c.1900.

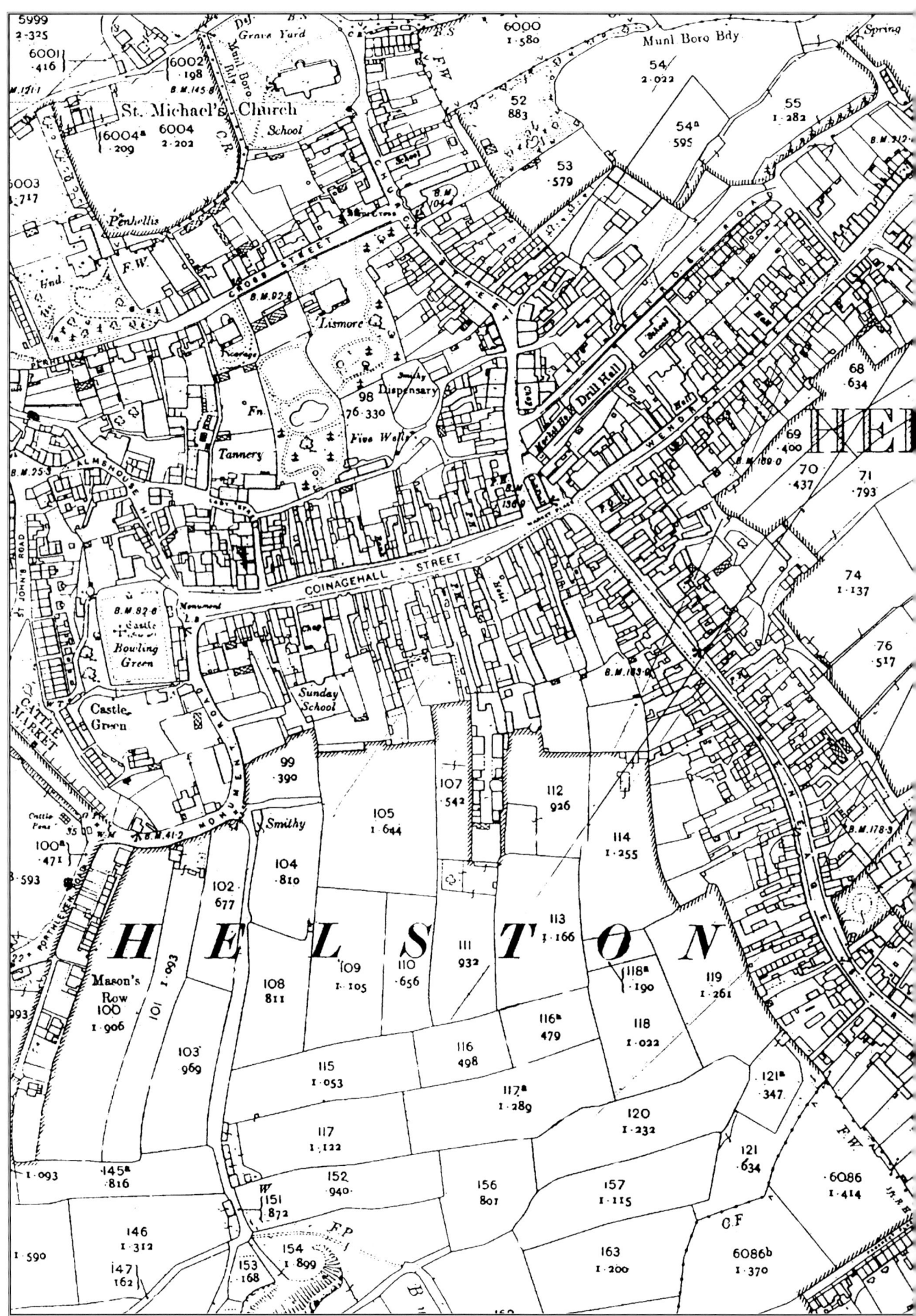

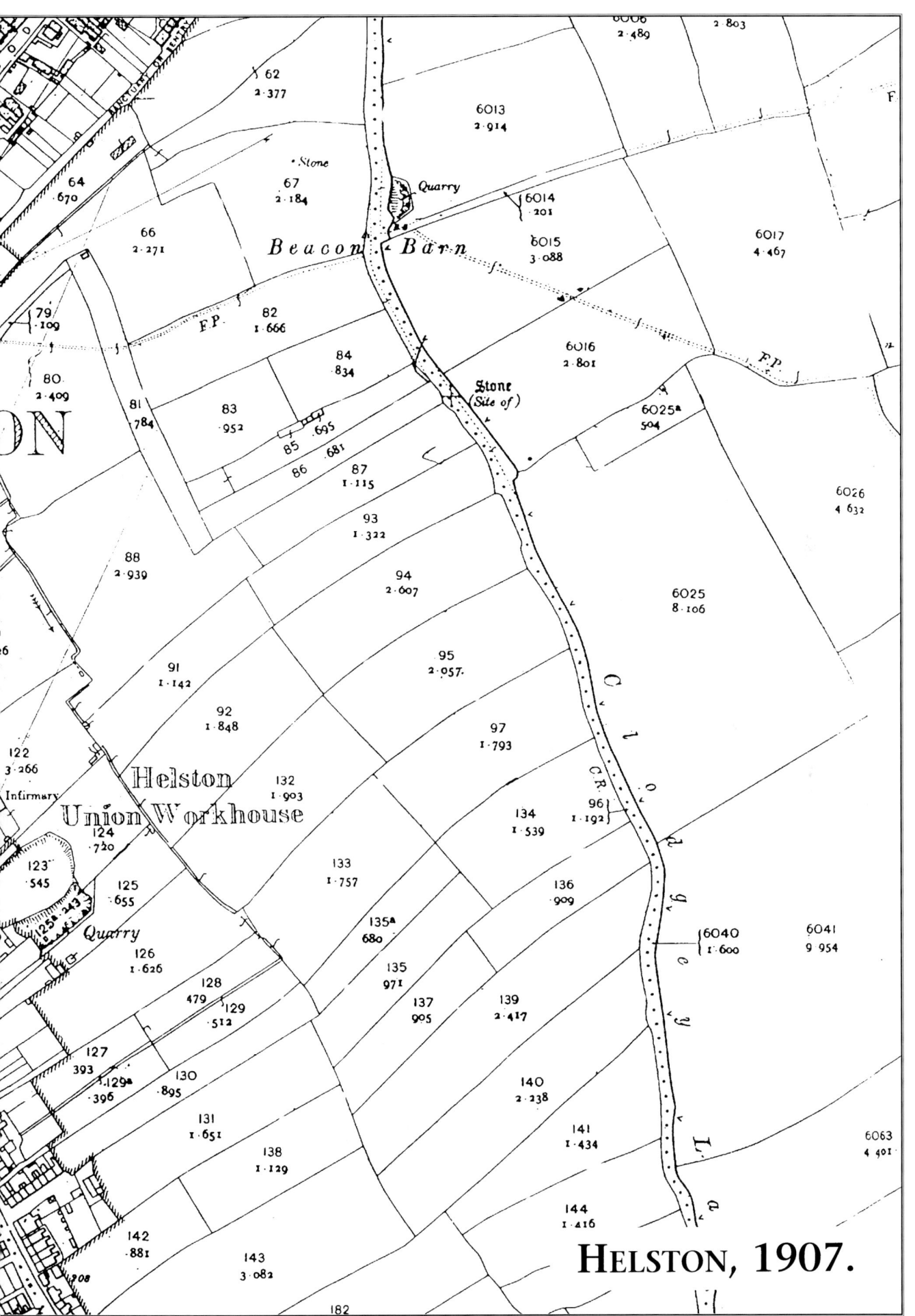

Lower Meneage Street, 1924, showing Kneebone's Chandlery and Leather Merchants. Mr Kneebone would cut out a pair of leather taps and supply the nails for customers wanting to mend their own shoes. The horse and cart is being driven by Ronnie Wearne, accompanied by Bill Rogers.

Market day in Helston, c.1920.

Chapter 2: Meneage Street and Around 1880–1920

At the crossroads of Church Street, Wendron Street, Meneage Street and Coinagehall Street there stands a fine block of buildings of granite ashlar, including the Guildhall. The ground upon which it is built used to be a market, and the area was called Market Place – an address still used by the Midland Bank.

In the 1830s the market house, which is featured in a beautiful watercolour in the museum, was removed and the Guildhall (opened in 1839) built on the cleared site. This incorporated the Corn Exchange, the Mayor's Parlour and Council Chamber. The foundation stone of the original market house dated 1576 was built into the end wall of the Corn Exchange. The slate face of an old clock, believed to have been that on the old market house, is in the museum. The pediment on the front of the Guildhall, a fine example of an early-Victorian public building, contains the armorial bearings of the town carved in Bath stone.

The steps on the east side of the Guildhall, known as Market Steps, lead down to New Market House, which was built in 1837–38 and where, for the next 100 years, a market was held every Saturday. The building was divided into two sections, namely the butter and egg market, with the meat market at the rear. The bell on its roof was rung to summon people to the market, and was also sounded towards the end of the day to indicate the closing of trade. With this warning sound in their ears, bargain hunters would rush to take advantage of the low prices to be had at the end of the day. In later years the bell was rung to summon the fire brigade. Since 1949 this building has been the town's museum and contains many exhibits relating to Helston and the surrounding area.

The gun outside the museum is from the wreck of the frigate *Anson*, which went ashore on the Loe Bar in 1807 with a considerable loss of life. The gun was retrieved from the sea bed by a team of naval divers and placed on display outside the museum in 1965.

The busy market scene, typical of the late 1800s, is recalled in an article by Mr W. J. Winn:

The [market's] higher part was occupied by the butchers and was known as the Meat Market. Every stall was occupied and many hundreds of crooks each held a joint, some large, some small. The Market of an evening about 7p.m. would be crowded with farmers and their wives, miners and their wives, and fishermen and theirs.

The lower half of the Market in the higher part was occupied by the Pork Hucksters. Then below them was Penaluna's gingerbread and sweet stall, on the south side and the other side tripe and cowheel vendors did a big trade. Below this and down to the market house gates were the farmer's wives with their... butter and eggs. In the level space outside the market house gates there would often be a Clome [china] Stall where plates and basins, etc. brought from the potteries enticed buyers.

In the Corn Market farmers occupied all the available space with sacks of corn which they had brought to town for sale on horseback or in light market carts. In front of the Corn Market in spring and early summer stood the agricultural seed merchant and opposite Mr Martyn's Shop a quack doctor could be seen with his bottled specimens of tapeworms, etc., and very often displaying life-size representations of the various internal organs of the human body whilst he glibly announced that his vegetable pills could cure every element that flesh is heir to.

In front of Mr Drew's Chemist's Shop (afterwards Wakeham) the Mayor and Mayoress of St Johns, Tommy and Mary Gilbert, sold rock, etc., and a little lower down Mr and Mrs Philpott sold home-made cinnamon rock.

From thence down the side of the street were about 15 to 18 Boot and Shoe stalls with small tables and a bit of carpet so that miners could try on their boots. On the south side of Coinagehall Street John Pryor, known as 'Apple John', offered the various fruits that were in season, and below him Mr Crapp Senior, Benny Barnes and Lawrence, the latter two hailing from Penzance district, sold vegetables, etc. All fruit and vegetables in those days were sold by measure rather than by weight (a gallon of potatoes, not 7lb bags)

Trigg women [trigging being the collection of cockles at low tide] offered their cockles, mussels and winkles. Vans and carts occupied the sides of the streets below the Angel, in Church Street and in Wendron Street and Meneage Street – in fact wherever there was stabling. In front of Reed and Roberts' Shop and the Duke's Head, Cooper Medlin had a stall on which various measures, butter prints, etc. were displayed. Then came a stall for the sale of rope, etc., kept by Mr S. Ellis and

50 YEARS IN MENEAGE STREET

Left: *Looking down Meneage Street, 1900. The brick building on the left was known as the doctor's house and is now occupied by Eddy & Sons. The town house on the right with the railings is now W.H.Smith.*

Right: *Meneage Street in 1910. Note the earth roads and open kennels. On the extreme right hand side is the water pump from which the townspeople drew their drinking water. The children in the middle, with their white collars, may well have come from the orphanage in Church Street.*

Left: *Wartime Meneage Street. Note the Army car coming up the road, and Eddys' shop replacing the Daton's house visible in the top picture.*

Right: *Meneage Street in 1950. Note the motorcycle side car coming up the street. The two-way system was still in operation and the kennels next to the tarmac road were covered. The Beringer clock shown in the top picture is now mounted above Mr Lee's shop.*

Meneage Street. (Courtesy Gerald Trethowan)

immediately above outside Mr Jas Woolcock's Shop Mary Allen of Porthleven and various others in the same line rent the air with their shouts of 'Now's your time! Mackerel as big as your leg; Pilchards five a penny, Buy a good hake Mister? Only 6d. for this one.'

Further up Meneage Street on the wide space outside the the Workhouse was the Pig Market where Henry Pascoe and John Retallack and others held squealing young porkers by their hind legs to give added length to their appearance.

The building to the left of the market entrance was at one time known as the Helston Public Subscription Rooms and housed the Trustee Savings Bank. It was moved from the Church Street building to Meneage Street at the bottom of Horse and Jockey Lane in the mid 1960s, to the shop now occupied by Stokes the greengrocers. The business expanded and TSB later moved lower down Meneage Street to be opposite the National Westminster Bank.

Meneage Street

Meneage Street, the second shopping area of town – Coinagehall Street being the first – was where I was born and spent much of my youth. The population of the street was at one time quite dense with many of the business families living above their shops or in the courts, of which there were quite a number. In addition there were also several fine houses with access to stabling and gardens at the rear. The ground floors of these larger houses were later turned into shops. In the 1930s new council houses were built in Bullock Lane and some of the courts cleared of families. After the war many more council houses were built.

Looking up Meneage Street from Lloyds Bank stands an empty shop which was last used as a fast-food restaurant and which has seen many different uses throughout the years. At the turn of the century it was part of the Globe Hotel and in my youth it was the site of Read & Roberts the drapers. Later, three cousins – two men and a lady – took it on and called it 'Cousins'. In 1967 it was divided into Johnnie Walker's chemists and a greengrocers. On the opposite corner where Yates, the house agents, now stands, was another chemists (*advertised above*) run by Mr J.B. Martin. Just before the Second World War it was taken over by Boots, and became the first chain store to open in the town. Mr Martin had a staff of four, the most notable being Dickie Gale, the dispenser. He had a good knowledge of the town, and whatever anybody wanted to know Dickie was always expected to provide an answer. The corner was a regular meeting place for people; for the middle years of the 20th century it was popularly known as Boot's Corner. Between the two world wars the regular meeting place was the opposite corner which was known as Cousins' Corner. The doorway offered shelter from the

Miss Edith Winn's shop.
Left to right: Kathleen Pascoe, Erna Jenkin, Miss Edith Winn. The entrance on the right of the shop lead to a cobbled court in which there were stables, James' bakery and Rogers the printers.

Curtis' Boot and Shoe Warehouse. Mr Curtis is on the right of the picture and Mr Sumpster (without a jacket) is in the centre. Note the fine example of contemporary gas lighting.

*Cousins staff, 1960. Left to right, back: Alfreda Pope, Iris Thomas, Muriel Adams;
centre: Mrs Wakeham, Shirley Addison, Jennifer Davies, Joan Kendall;
front: Mable Anthony (kneeling), Miss Irene Brown.*

weather especially on Saturday nights for those awaiting the arrival at 9.30p.m. of the *Evening Herald* football paper which listed all of the local football results and enjoyed a large following in those days before local radio.

The greengrocers, next to the newly-opened estate agents, is now a book shop with the Stead and Simpson shoe shop as its neighbour. The former occupies a site which was once the old Post Office, and which before this was a public house called the Duke's Head Inn, run by the Symons family (no relation to the shoemakers). Mr Symons also owned a brewery and another inn down Coinagehall Street. In my youth, my sister Erna used to work in the ladies millinery shop, which is now part of Stead and Simpson. This was owned by Miss Winn, who was a daughter of Mr W. J. Winn. Before being taken on by Miss Winn the property belonged to Miss Lander, one of my mother's cousins.

At the end of the war when I was demobbed and came home with my young wife, Inger, Miss Winn kindly offered us the chance of living above her shop. So, for a number of years, Inger and I lived in this flat in the heart of Helston and it was from here that our daughter Suzanne was born. Immediately next door was an entrance to a cobbled court in which there were stables belonging to the Duke's Head, together with a courtyard where Mr Rogers senr had his first printers before he moved to Church Street. There was also a bakehouse belonging to Edwin James, who had his shop across the street. Mr Leonard Oliver also had his first paint shop there. This court was of great historical interest but sadly the Town and District Councils seemed not to appreciate the value of it from an historical point of view as they removed the court's opening to make it part of the Stead and Simpson shoe shop. With foresight this could have been made into a very attractive arcade of small shops.

Warren's the bakers used to be a grocery shop run by the chain store Home & Colonial. Originally it was a drapers shop run by the Rapson family, who at one time lived where the NatWest bank now stands. The furniture shop traded as 'James' for many years. Where the butchers shop is now, was, during the 1920s, a leather shop belonging to Mr Kneebone who repaired boots and shoes and worked as a saddler. At this time it was common practice for many people to carry out their own boot and shoe repairs and Mr Kneebone would sell the leather for this purpose. In fact, if one went in with a pair of shoes, he would cut out a pair of taps and supply the nails and wherewithall for the do-it-yourself type person to complete the repair. His son, Harold, was very clever with his hands and made the mechanical, chiming Flora-Day carousel which is kept in the museum in Market Place. Across the street above Boots Corner was Mr Charles Oliver's

Top: *The estate agents, once a chemists.*
Above: *Modern-day shops in Lower Meneage Street.*

butchers shop, with Mr Hawke the photographer as an immediate neighbour above the shop.

This part of town once boasted a fine array of small shops housing family businesses. H.A.L. Rowe supplied ironmongery to Helston inhabitants for over 100 years, and the outside of the building did not alter until Mr Denis Williams, the grandson, sold out during the mid 1990s. In contrast the neighbouring shop has been witness to several owners and many different uses during the last century. A large clock used to hang outside the building when Mr Beringer the jeweller was in business there and in the days before radio this clock was very useful to townsfolk as a time check. Later the shop was occupied by Mrs Gulliford, the greengrocer. When she moved out just before the Second World War the Cornwall Electrical Power Company moved in from Church Street and established a new showroom, later to become SWEB. Gerald Sampson recalls:

When I started to work for the Cornwall Electrical Power Company, they had a shop in Church Street, which is still there, but which is now empty. There is a lane going up the side of it and up this lane used to be a shed which was the stores where all the men congregated, picked up their kit and went about their various jobs. Vallie Oates was the office chief and only clerk, Geoff Banks was foreman electrician, whose father had worked for the electricity board before, and there was one electrician, Albert Thomas, who is still living in Porthleven, with his apprentice Binnie Andrews. I was taken on as an apprentice at 18, three years later than normal. The man I was allocated to work with was Edward Williams also from Porthleven. His father was a fisherman and he later went back and joined him. I wired the shop in Meneage Street, which was a greengrocer's shop, and became the company showrooms.

When I was a boy the shop which is now W.H. Smith was a large private house with railings along the front and up to the front door. Viewed from the other side of the street one can still appreciate the grandeur of this old town house. The Kirby family who owned it were valuers, auctioneers, etc., in the days before Mr Carah came there to live and ran a dentist's surgery. Later he moved to a surgery over Perry's China Shop which was the site where Boots is now. Mr Luke, who later ran Toy's Foundry, moved into the house vacated by Mr Carah whilst Mr Luke was having a house built in Meneage Road. When he moved out, it ceased being Milford House. Mr A.P. Gilbert the ironmonger took it on, he had the iron railings removed, all the granite front knocked down, and put in the shop entrance. In the basement of the house he put in a large paraffin storage tank, which was filled regularly from a bowser parked out in the street. Hundreds of gallons of paraffin were pumped into the tank beneath the shop although fire regulations would never allow this today.

Across the road and one door up from Mr Hawke's photographic shop was Edwin James' bakery. When he first started baking, his bakehouse was on the opposite side of the road in a court which opened onto the road next to Miss Winn's shop. The bakers used to bring all the bread down to the shop using handbarrows. Some time later Mr James had a new bakehouse built in the back of the shop. Edwin's father was Peter James, a master cabinet maker, who had a workshop in Shute Hill where he made 'jingles' or traps. He also kept a horse-drawn hearse which he rented out to undertakers in the town.

Top: *Post Office staff pictured during the mayoral Christmas visit. Included are: William Kempthorne, ? Roberts, ? Whatmore, Jackett Simpson, Willy Pascoe, D. Trevorrow, Sid Hendy, Mr Penham, A.H. Pascoe, Guy Rich, Mrs Cox, Dr Michael, Joe Thomas, ? Hendy, N. Ellis, Miss Letcher, Mrs Rogers, W.J. Rogers (Mayor).*
Above: *Curnow's Confectioners, 15 Meneage Street, which is now occupied by Wearne's the jewellers.*

What is now Thurley's Fish and Chip Shop has had the same use for many years. I first knew it as Pascoe's Fish and Chip Shop, when it had a coal-fired fryer. As young lads, we used to go in there on Tuesday nights after first-aid tuition at the ambulance station. One of the daughters was called Ada and had a reputation as being something of a 'sergeant major'; she wouldn't have any nonsense with anybody and if we made too much noise in the café, she would come down and tell us to be quiet or get out of the premises. Mr Pascoe was a very pleasant, comfortable man, from Porthleven. His first wife died, and he married a Mrs Colenso whose son Fred eventually took over the shop. In December 1980 there was a severe fire and much of the building and the premises next door were badly damaged. Thanks to prompt action by the fire-brigade, and to the improved building regulations which had been taken into account during alterations, the damage was not as great as it might have been. The chip shop and what is now the Abbey National Building Society were re-furbished in the traditional style of the street almost to their original appearance.

Next up the road was Tyacks, formerly J.B. Gilbert's paper and stationery shop which Miss Barker took on after moving from the present-day site of the Midland Bank. Then came Reeds & Nicholls' seed and forage merchant's shop run by Mr George Nicholls and his staff, among them Mr Perry and Miss Jenkin. Mr Perry became a war reserve constable during the Second World War. Mr Nicholls was a tall and rather smart gentleman who lived over the shop with his sister. The building became Liptons after the Second World War and is now the store McKays.

Brewer's Court is one of the last remaining courts in Meneage Street and it is here that Mr Sam Brewer started his printing works. His son Clifford then took it on, and now his grandsons run a large printing business at the Water-ma-Trout Industrial Estate.

The shop which is now Eddy & Sons was for 100 years known as the doctor's house. Dr J.P. Michael was the last doctor to live in this beautiful brick-fronted building and Eddy & Sons bought the premises in 1936 when Dr Michael moved to 'Lismore' in Cross Street. At the back of the house there were stables (although the traps had to be left out in the road). On the left hand side of Eddy's is a small toy shop which used to belong to Mr Ireland the dentist. This gentleman had a treadle machine that he used to power his tools and which is now in the museum. The shop next door was where Mr Curtis had a wonderful range of boots and shoes. Next to that is a building with the name WALTER fashioned in the concrete on the wall. At one time this was yet another premises selling shoes and is now Ward's flower shop.

The next building up (now NatWest Bank) was a lovely family town house owned by the Rapson family who kept a drapers shop next to Miss Winn's (where they lived beforehand). The family eventually moved to Godolphin Road. Lloyds Bank then took over their grand house as a business premises and stayed there until their move, in 1909, to Market Place, where they remain. The National Provincial Bank then took over the building, the manager of which had a large chow dog which everybody in the street was frightened of. In 1950 the banking firm removed the upstairs bay window to make the building look more like a bank and less like a private residence.

Next to this is the Rodney Pub, once kept by the Oates family, before the Shillabeers arrived in 1928. They stabled horses at the back and would leave the traps in the street before walking the horses right down through the pub to the back. The same method was used in the Bell next door! Across the street, where Millers the estate agents are now, lived the three Miss Jennings, one of whom was the manageress at Reed and Roberts, whilst the other two made their living through millinery and dressmaking. They had a large bay window in which they would sit with the curtains drawn back so that they could look up and down the street, and everybody could look in. In front

---

H. A. L. ROWE,
General Furnishing & Builder's Ironmonger
Plumber, Tinplate Worker, & Bell Hanger,
MENEAGE STREET, HELSTON.

Estimates given for all kinds of work.

Bedsteads, Baths, Cisterns, Lamps, Tile Register Grates
Electro-plated Goods, Cutlery, etc., in great variety.
A Good Stock of Sanitary Fittings always in stock.

S. STRIKE & A. A. CHEGWIDDEN,
Beg to inform the inhabitants of Helston and Neighbourhood, that they have Commenced Business as

Machine & Letter-press Printers,
MENEAGE ST., HELSTON,
And hope by strict attention to Business to merit a share of public patronage.

BOOKBINDING IN ALL ITS BRANCHES.
All Orders Promptly attended to.

BENNETTS & SON,
Music Warehouse, HELSTON.
PIANOFORTES, HARMONIUMS, AMERICAN ORGANS.
Tuning and Repairing a Speciality.
Agents for "His Master's Voice" Gramophone Records and Accessories. Also "Winner," "Regal" and "V.F." Records Stocked.

of the window was a table with a silver tea service on it which they would make a great show of using for their afternoon tea. We used to refer to the trio as the 'Silver Service Sisters' – and individually as 'Milk Jug', 'Sugar Basin' and 'Teapot'. Despite this teasing, we found them to be very nice. Their father was a cabinet maker who had a business at the rear and later the site was turned into a greengrocers shop. It is now Millers Estate Agents.

Next along the street there was a small shop which used to sell drapery and which is now a sweet shop. Beyond that was the home and office of the Registrar of Births, Deaths and Marriages, Mr Cade. When he moved out, Dickie Gale moved in. The building is now Threshers, the wine shop. The next shop up (Lloyds T.S.B.), belonged to Mr Lee the jeweller. At the base of the building is a bench mark with a height above sea level of approximately 150 feet. Mr Lee started his business in Church Street, and was the first man to have electricity in Helston. He had his own generator at the back of the house and illuminated his window at night. As youngsters it gave us great pleasure to go down and gaze in through the lit-up glass.

Next door was Alfred Lawrence's Fish and Chip Shop, which is now Ruth's Cafe and Bread Shop. Alfred had been in business with his brothers as builders and masons and when he opened his new shop it contained a gleaming coal-fired fish fryer. His wife and son Cyril helped in the business, and when his parents died, Cyril continued it for many years, building up a good reputation in the town. What is now the video shop was the music shop of Mr Fred Bennett, whose daughter, Geraldine, ran a hairdressers at the back of the building. Fred sold pianos and musical instruments, but also tuned pianos, sold music of all descriptions and taught young people to play – not only the piano, but a variety of other musical instruments as well. He also re-charged accumulators for battery radios.

Next was the saddlery shop. I remember the name on the facia board as being 'Harris' and that on the window light being 'Hendy'. Mr Hendy was in there in 1926 and afterwards Mr Lay took over the business and continued to employ Edgar Angove, a deaf and dumb man called Lindsay, and a third man – all making saddlery. When Mr Lay retired the Gilberts took over and continued to run it as a saddlery for a while until the trade declined and they turned to selling travelling cases, handbags and sportswear. This shop was on the corner of Horse and Jockey Lane. Right outside the door, but in the lane itself, was a hand

Middle Meneage Street The clock belonging to A.E. Lee the jeweller is still on the Beringer building down the street; the shop with the gas street light in front is Gilberts the ironmongers.

pump, from which a great many of the people living in the surrounding area used to get their water.

Leading off to the left of Meneage Street about half way up is Horse and Jockey Lane. This was never a public lane; there were double doors at the bottom and these were opened on Mondays and Saturdays to allow horses and carts to go and park in the fields above. The stables, off to the left at the top of the lane, were owned by the Prisk family, the landlords of the Horse & Jockey Inn. Mr Barzillai Thomas, who kept (and lived above) the drapers shop across the street, leased the stables and kept his horse and carriage there. Mr Thomas was one of the most significant employers in Helston. He ran a high-class tailoring, dress-making and hat-making business, in addition to selling millinery and the latest ladies' fashions. Some of his apprentices in tailoring and haberdashery later migrated to London. After the Second World War the shop was taken over by Dingles of Plymouth, and later by House of Frazer.

The Horse & Jockey Inn stood where the fruit shop is now, next to Boots. The original inn was torn down when the new shop, later to become the china shop of W.R. Perry, was built. Mr Perry also had the grocers next door (where Superdrug is now) and had a horse and cart as well as two vans which were used for grocery deliveries all over the area. He kept his vehicles behind the double doors between his two shops.

Harry Perry's Rock Shop, at No. 44 Meneage Street, was just a front room with the rock-making facility at the back, but he also ran a regular market stall on Saturdays near the Guildhall, and he had a regular stand at the tea treats throughout the Lizard peninsula. It was beautiful stuff; we used to go on Saturdays and get a pennyworth of broken rock splinters. Above the shop lived the Downing family who had come from Bullock Lane. The daughters worked at Lizard Laundry, Skyburriowe, and travelled out and back each day by bus. Walter Downing drove a GWR lorry delivering goods in the area.

In the house next door (now the Card Shop) lived the Downing family (no relation to above),

and at No. 48 (in what is now Mr C. Bloor's jewellery shop) 'Barber' Cooke used to hold forth. A Mawgan man, he was related to the builder brothers and lived over the shop. He used to give tuppeny haircuts but as boys we only paid a penny. He was always busy, especially on Saturdays, and although it was not the cleanest of places, he made a go of it and provided plenty of chat and gossip – old and new.

Next to Barber Cooke's where there was once the dentist but which is now a solicitor's office, there lived a Mr Woods who worked in the bank. He had a daughter called, Margaret, and two sons, Irving and John – John went to Australia to live. The adjacent shop, where Rowes the bakers is now, was originally Willy Pearce's saddlery. Willy moved from there to the other side of the road, and Joe Pascoe came in from Porthleven to run a boot and shoe shop. It was here, as a ten-year-old, that I had my first job as errand boy, delivering and collecting shoes for 2 shillings a week. The house next door was where Mr Jack Hitchens, the painter and decorator, had his paint shop. He took out the front window and replaced it with one large single pane of glass and turned the front room into a shop.

One further up the street was the printers, Strike & Chegwidden (both Porthleven men), who took over the business from a Mr Woolcock. Later Gus Proctor moved in and carried on the printing. Behind Chegwidden's was Woolcock's Court – once containing six houses, two of which were reached via their own steps, with the toilets across the cobbled yard. This has all gone now, but it was here that Mr Wear and his family lived and where Ward's flower shop (owned by Noel Thomas) was for some time. Ernie and Selina Whiffing had their tobacconists shop (*above*) where Nigel Williams now has his butchers. Next door to this lived a painter and decorator by the name of Uren, whose cottage has remained largely unchanged. The cobbled opening next to what is now the sports shop leads up to a cottage (still in existence) where my brother John was born in 1913. The sports shop itself used to be a farmhouse occupied by the farmer Mr Jeffery (whose housekeeper was Mrs Weekes). Denis Williams recalls that as a boy

MIDDLE MENEAGE STREET

Photographs clockwise from left: Queenie Bassett, wife of Nelson, with her milk float; Pascoe's Cycle Shop on fire in 1928. The boy in the background is believed to be Percy Jenkin; Pascoe's Cycle Shop again, on the site of the old farm in Meneage Street which supplied milk and cream to the area. The opening on the left leads to a cottage where John Jenkin was born; Mrs Lugg's Victorian-built shop with Chipman Court to the left. The shop remained intact until the 1980s and was a small general provisions store with a lovely smell of spices and ground coffee. A replica can be seen at Flambards' Victorian Village.

E. DUNSTAN,
MENEAGE STREET, HELSTON,
AND AT PORTHLEVEN.
Tailor, Hatter, and Outfitter,
Ready-made Clothing. Gloves, Scarfes, Umbrellas, Hosiery
Hunting Suits, Riding Breeches, Uniforms.
Liveries to order. Waterproof Garments and Leather Leggings
Felt & Silk Hats from Best Makers. Bunting Flags on hire.

JOHN TOY,
Iron & Brass Founder, Helston.
Plumbing in all its Branches by Competent Workmen.
Baths, Lavatories, Water Closets, etc.
Electric Bell Installations (with or without Indicators), a Speciality. Telephones, etc.
Cooking Ranges of all sizes, and fitted with welded Steel high pressure Boilers, for Hot and Cold Water Services to Baths, Lavatories, etc.
Hydraulic Rams & Water Wheels, fitted with force pumps Pumps of all kinds. Warranted of Best Make, and kept in repair for Six Months if fixed by my own Men.
Estimates given free, and all Orders for New Work or Repairs, in Town or Country, promptly attended to.
Old Copper, Brass, Lead, Iron, &c., purchased at Best Market Prices

he often purchased cream from the dairy when the pans of separated milk stood on slate slabs. Off the cobbled court was a barn where the corn and cattle feed were stored, and higher up towards what is now Trengrouse Way Car Park were the pig pens.

At the back of No. 62, there is a big wooden building which used to be the brewery where my father was foreman. It was run either by Mr Sleeman, or Mr Jeffery; both came from the same family and were originally from Gweek where they ran a coal business. A right turn off the court led into the back entrance of 64 Meneage Street – the home of Mrs H.A.L. Rowe whose daughter Marjory married a Williams from Gweek. The couple emigrated to Australia where their son Denis was born; sadly the father died and Denis and his mother came back to Helston. They lived for some time with Mrs Rowe, and then Marjory married Mr Hill at the Lizard and went out there to live. Denis stayed with his grandmother, went to Helston County Secondary School and later took on the ironmongers business. When he married Kay they continued to live in the same house, next door to my brother John, until moving out to Gillan. At that time the house was sold and turned into an antiques shop. Next door is the home of my brother John and is where Maud Pearce once lived with her daughter Lillian. Maud worked at B. Thomas', the drapery, and Lillian worked as a clerk in the Town Office at the Guildhall before eventually marrying and emigrating, before the war, to Zimbabwe (then Rhodesia). She is still living in Harare, and I hear from her occasionally. She must be a woman coming up to 90 and her husband, who was a Breage man called Stephens, is still living. We, the Jenkin family, lived next door at No. 68. I was born at No. 98, but Percy (two years younger) was born in 68. This is where I spent my childhood and youth.

When I was a boy we never had the luxury of water closets. They were all earth closets which had to be emptied – a lengthy and unpleasant task which was usually done in the winter. The sewerage scheme was introduced in the late 1920s and I remember men coming and digging all the way down Meneage Road and Meneage Street to put in the pipes. In Lady Street the houses were so close together that the pipes had to be placed very deep indeed and a great many Welsh and Irish men came to help with the work. They put a hole down outside Leslie House, and dug away underneath until they came up opposite the Blue Anchor, thus crossing the road without digging it up. In 1930 Mr W.J. Winn wrote:

Top: *The Staff of Pearce's saddlery.*
The photograph includes Mr Pearce, Bill Triggs, Beattie Pearce, W. Pearce and Mrs Pearce senr.
Above: *Helston Toc H 1937.*
Included in the picture are Ken Hinks, Percy Charles, Joe Walters, Garth Thomas and Joe Rowe.

Only a little time before my birth (1848) Helston was visited by that terrible scourge Cholera which decimated the population. Then, in 1858, there was an epidemic of scarlet fever which caused the death of a great many of the young folk. 12 or 13 years after that we were ravaged by smallpox [which] caused death and disfigurement to a great number. People began asking themselves whether these things could be prevented or were they due to circumstances over which we had no control? The reply was not far to seek. The population of the borough was just over 4000, but a high proportion of these dwelt in small, closely packed buildings in cobbled courts. These 'Courtlages' were teeming with life and also teeming with filth. Closets were in close proximity to the cottages and the occupants of these cottages conserved their filth until they had accumulated sufficient to induce some farmer to purchase it for manure. Is it to be wondered that trouble so invited should materialize? We invariably reap according to our sowing. For half a century we talked about drainage, now I am happy seeing something done. Costly it may be... but health in my judgement stands higher than £.s.d.

Across the street almost opposite Boots was Wearne's the bakers, originally owned by Josiah Roberts – well renowned for the quality of his saffron cakes. He had a sister, Jane, who married William Nicholls of Manaccan. The building is now the Horse and Jockey Pastry Shop, which started its business in Horse and Jockey Lane. Down at the back with the bakehouse were two tennis courts and during Harvest Fair wrestling matches were held in the field alongside the courts. The shop which is now Davies, the solicitors, was Mr Leonard Oliver's paint shop. On the side of it was an arcade that had a sliding door. One used to be able to go through there, over a footbridge and into Mr Hawke's former studio. Next door to that was Miss Lugg's grocer's – she was there for a lifetime and many of her old fittings are now in Flambards Victorian Village. Down through this opening was Chipman's Court where two or three families lived. The large granite post in the middle of the opening was put there as a bar to vehicles. Next door to this was a little private house where Albert Symonds lived, with Mr Addison, the barber, one door further up the

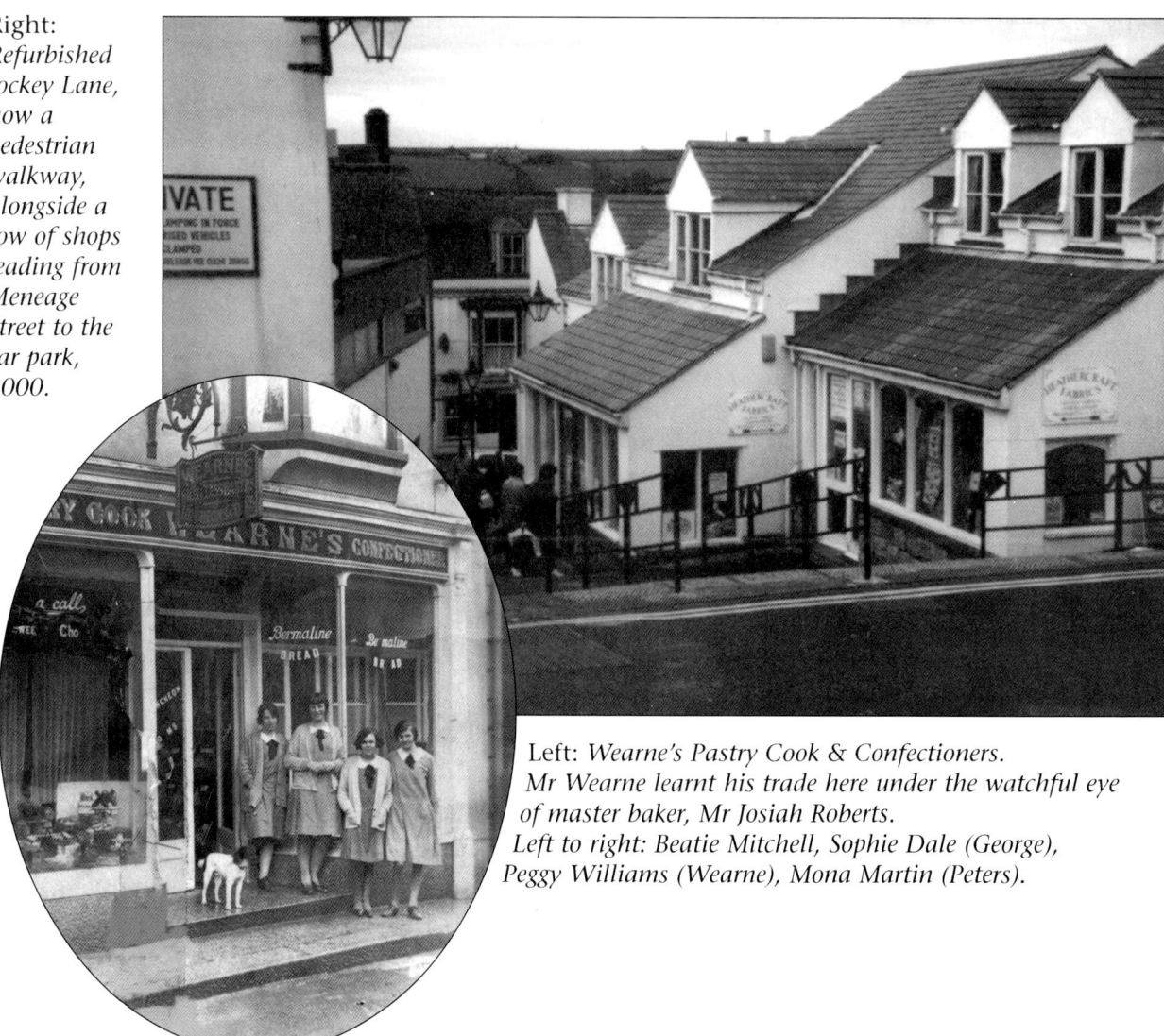

Right: *Refurbished Jockey Lane, now a pedestrian walkway, alongside a row of shops leading from Meneage Street to the car park, 2000.*

Left: *Wearne's Pastry Cook & Confectioners. Mr Wearne learnt his trade here under the watchful eye of master baker, Mr Josiah Roberts. Left to right: Beatie Mitchell, Sophie Dale (George), Peggy Williams (Wearne), Mona Martin (Peters).*

street. He was a short portly man reputed to be a rapid and expert shaver.

Next door to this was Pyatt's brush shop, which sold nothing but brushes of all shapes and sizes and which was later owned by the Moyle family. Next up was Willy Pearce's saddlery. Bill Triggs who worked for him was one of Helston's great characters. Next to him was Mrs Trezise and her daughter Bessie who sold dress material, needles, pins, etc., together with groceries, tea, sugar, coffee and so on. No matter what you wanted they had it.

When he first came to Helston, Mr A.P. Gilbert set up his ironmongers in the building next door to Trezise's shop, with his living accommodation on the first floor. (Later he moved lower down the street to No. 20.). Here there is an opening down to Meneage Yard which provided more parking for horses. Next door to this and before Meneage House was Joe Pentecost's fruit and vegetable shop. Meneage House itself (63 Meneage Street) belonged to an ex-gold-miner, Mr Bolitho, who lived there for well over 30 years. The building remains relatively unchanged although the double-fronted dwelling house next to this, No. 65, was made into a small shop with an office alongside which housed the leather sales shop of Cunnacks tanners and leather merchants, and which is was subsequently occupied by H.G. Oliver, butcher, delicatessen and wine sales. South of the opening to the yard was where the Cunnack family had their drying sheds for hides used in the tannery, and beyond that a Mr and Mrs Harry Clifton had a greengrocers – Mr Clifton offered a delivery service for his customers with a horse and wagon which were housed in a shed at the rear of the shop.

To the south of this is the entrance to what was Mr Eathorne's yard, where the Toc H building used to be. Mr Eathorne, a Constantine man and a fruit merchant, lived in the large double-fronted house with his wife – No. 69 (which was, until the late-20th century, Gallery Arts). He had a wooden leg which somewhat restricted his movements but he could still ride in a pony and trap and he ran a very successful business, selling apples, gooseberries, raspberries and various other fruits. He had two or three men working for him full time in his two shops and at blackberry time would buy all of the berries picked around the area – many of them from the gypsies who brought them in by the cartload in wickerwork mawns. From here they went to a jam factory at Redruth. He was certainly at an advantage; being the only person who would buy the berries he could dictate his own price and was a very keen businessman. As boys the ripe fruit in the fields up behind our house was a great temptation and occasionally we used to scrump a few gooseberries or strawberries off his land. He had three children, a son called Rodney and two daughters, one of whom married a Mr Dunn of Newham Farm. The second girl also married (although to whom is not known) and moved away.

Next door to Mr Eathorne's was a smaller house inhabited by Mr and Mrs Hearty Peters – Mrs Peters was the daughter of Mr Walters at the shoe shop in Meneage Street. Beyond this were two shops occupied by Mr W. Johns the baker, whose bakery was in Prospect Place. The house next to Mr Johns was occupied by Mr Jack Walters and family whilst one door on from that was a general grocers which was taken over by a Mr Dale and Mr Martin after the Second World War and turned into an electrical appliance shop.

Phyllis Walters' one-time home later became Leslie Pascoe's Pork Shop where one could buy delightful skinless sausages by the pound. A row of five were laid out on floured grease-proof paper, followed on top by four, three and two to create a sausage pyramid with a shake of flour between each layer. The hog's pudding was also excellent. Later, Scorse's took the shop over as a butchers. Another butchers, run by the Lenderyou family at 75 Meneage Street, was, I think, the home of Jack Walters who worked for many years as a chauffeur for Sir Montague Rogers at Nansloe. Jack was a Liberal and his employer a Conservative. One year, at election time, Sir Montague chose to take out the carriage and horses decorated in Conservative colours and Jack refused to comply; he received his marching orders forthwith as employees were expected to vote the way of their bosses. Wisely, Jack then went and worked for Sir Henry Toy, a Liberal.

My father's first wife was born at 77 Meneage Street (the Pharmacy) where the Symon's family also once had their shoe shop. In the 1881 census, Mr Symons was described as a 'Farmer and Cordwainer' and there was a farm down the back into which his wife used to drive the cattle from Clodgey Lane to be milked.

Right: *Woolcock's Court. In 1881 eight families lived here. Later it was roofed and became part of Ward's Florist Shop. The owner, Noel Thomas, kept an aquarium there.*

Above: *A cast-iron pump in the wall at Lismore. The pump was probably made at one of the town's foundries.*

Below: *The lift pump at the bottom of Horse and Jockey Lane which provided water for the residents of Middle Meneage Street until the mid 1920s.*

~ WATER ~

The availability of clean water had a very large part to play in the health of the nation. Piped water did not come to many homes in Helston until the mid 1930s. In 1926 a number of families were fortunate enough to be supplied with water from a reservoir at Tregathenan, Sithney, the property of the Helston and Porthlevan Water Company, but a vast majority of families drew their water from various wells throughout the town.

Most of these have now disappeared, but there is a cast-iron lift pump situated in the wall of Lismore House in Cross Street and of course the water still runs freely from Mayor Cock's Well, dated 1703, in Five Wells Lane.

It is interesting to note that when the Americans came to look for water to supply their troops leaving Trebah for Omaha, they found an adequate supply at Helford Passage, but declared it unfit for human consumption. The water had been drunk for generations by the locals, who had built up a resistance to the Cornish bugs. All of the water for the troops was specially piped in from Kergilliack near Falmouth.

Above: *Mayor Cock's Well, an open spring.*

Top: *Lift pump in Wendron Street outside the entrance to the Salvation Army Hall.*

Above: *The well at Helston Turnpike was fitted with a wheel and axle and supplied the people of Winns Row with water.*

❦ SUPPLY ❦

The wells throughout the town were of three main types:

1. *Lift pumps made of cast iron in one of the local foundries using leather washers from the Helston tanning industry;*
2. *Wheel-and-axle pumps using a bucket and rope;*
3. *Free-running water from a local spring.*

The wheel-and-axle pumps were very simple and consisted of an axle and a cranked handle. All were locally made. The wells served as a gathering point for occasional chat as people collected their water in buckets or pitchers. Eventually all of the wells were condemned because the water was declared unfit for human consumption – even for the hardy Cornish!

Trengrouse Way and The House Next Door

Next door to my boyhood home, on the corner of Trengrouse Way, was Pascoe's Cycle Shop (and before that a basket shop) which back then had a thatched roof.

Fridays was a hectic day for my mother. She always used to get up early and take out the oven for cleaning before breakfast. She would then clean out the soot from the flues and put the oven back in place. After breakfast she would black lead the grate, polish the brass and then scrub the granite floor from the back door through the kitchen, down the hallway and out over the front steps. After dinner on Fridays she spent her time baking ready for the weekend.

In Easter week 1935 she didn't take the oven out on Good Friday as was her usual custom and so rose early on Easter Sunday to complete the task. Her usual method was to take out the rings, put a paraffin rag on the top of the oven and set it alight to burn off the excess soot. Unfortunately on this occasion it set fire to the chimney and the sparks landed up on the thatched roof next door. I ran up to Jory's garage (where Helston Garages are now), as they had one of the only available phones in the place and called for the fire brigade. We tried to put out the fire using a hose connected to a tap, but of course eventually it all burned down. We saved a number of bicycles and then got told off by George Pascoe for having saved them: 'You should have left them all in there, and let them all burn!' he shouted. The shop was rebuilt and became the same old store once again and is now the fruit shop, run by Pauline Wills (née Ferris).

Between our house and the shop was a gateway leading to a cobbled back entrance. Up the back was an old house, belonging, like many other Helston properties, to the Penrose Estate. This house was used as a store where estate workers kept their ladders, cement, lime, etc. and there was also a pit there in which lime was quenched (slaked by adding water). The lime used to be put into the pit in blocks, water was poured onto it and when it was really boiling, oil was added to it to let the oil emulsify the lime ready for lime-washing the buildings. At 68 Meneage Street we added ochre to the mixture to give it a light saffron colour. Before the days when the Penrose Estate house became a store, an old lady lived there who one day came to my mother asking for advice. In her bag she had a rabbit which she needed some help with: 'I've been all the morning plucking this rabbit and I can't get the hair off of it', she complained – Mother had to set to and show her how to skin it!

The next house fronting Cades Yard was Jose Collins' auctioneers, where Jose Collins and Willy Collins had their office and stores. The entrance to Cades Yard was just wide enough to get a cart up and two local taxis used to be parked up there, belonging to Joe Blatchford and Joe White. The man who looked after Cades Yard was Albert Symons who had a big family and whose son, Harry, was a great friend of mine. Next to Collins' shop, which used to be supervised by Edgar Simmons (from Manaccan), was an opening leading to stables in Rodney Yard. Here horses and traps coming into town – especially on Saturdays – were looked after by Johnnie Williams. He lived in the next house and immediately adjacent were my grandparents (Mr and Mrs John James), whose home was attached to the wall of the Union building. When they died their son, John James the postman, lived there until the house was demolished to make room for Trengrouse Way.

Above: *Trengrouse Way in 1968 with Pascoe's Pork Shop behind the bollard. This building was the home of Jack Walters, the chauffeur for Sir Montague Rogers of Nansloe and later Sir Henry Toy.*

Right: *The bottom of Trengrouse Way in 1998 by which time Pascoe's had become Cornish Collectables, the china shop. The pharmacy (No. 77) is where Reg Jenkin's father's first wife was born. The Information Centre was home to Frank Pill, the area agent for the Redruth Brewery and the owner of the large yard next door, now part of Helston Garages.*

The Workhouse (or Union)

No. 78a Menage Street was the official address of the Poor Law Institution, otherwise known as the 'Union'. Entrance to the building was through a pair of double gates, on the left hand side of which is a spout from which water flowed continuously. A small area of the street had been cobbled at this point and the Post Office vans were brought there on Saturday mornings for washing and cleaning. At the far end of the boundary wall was another hand pump from which the local residents drew their water. Granny and Grandpa James got their water from here, as did the Williamses et al.

Amidst the cobbles there are four pieces of granite driven into the ground, two either side of the gateway and between which an iron bar was once curved in an arch – a structure which it is thought may have some connection with Helston Cattle Market. Before the First World War people brought along their cattle and tied them up hoping for a sale, a practice which developed into a formal cattle market at the bottom of town. Pigs meanwhile were kept in boxes.

The Workhouse was a hospital for elderly people and a home for children whose parents who could not afford to keep them. Unmarried mothers invariably went there to have their babies, who would be registered at that address. There were also many tramps who would come and queue up outside at 4.30p.m. each day ready to be let in to sleep for the night and to be given breakfast next morning. They would then work until 10.30a.m. when the gates would release them on to the streets once again.

In Canon Doble's book *Two Cornish Parishes – Wendron and Sithney in the Eighteenth Century*, there is an extract from the Overseers Book of 1755 for Wendron parish. It reads:

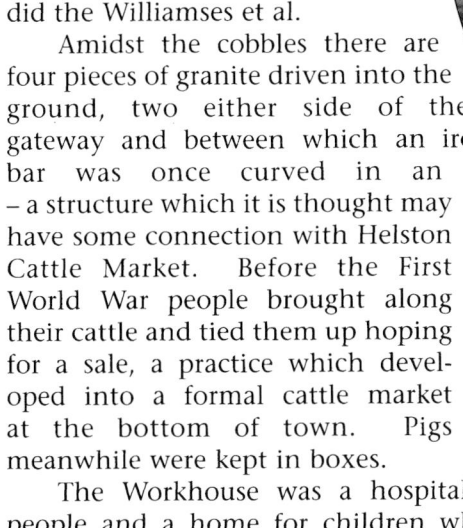

Above: *Mr and Mrs W.J. Perrin, Governor and Matron of the Poor Law Institution, 1920s.*

Below: *The building during conversion into modern housing, 1999.*

Take Notice that a Vestry will be held in the Parrish house of this Parrish on tuesday next being the 27th day of May instant by three o'Clock in the Afternoon where the Principal Inhabitants of this Parrish are desired to attend to consider some method for the better Provision of the poor and the ease of the Parrish

WHEREAS a Proposal has been made for severall Parrishes and Towns within the Hundreds of Penwith and Kirrier in this County to unite in hiring a convenient house for the lodging, keeping and maintaining the poor of the severall Parrishes and Towns so uniting AND WHEREAS a new erected house at Helstone fit and convenient for the said purposes is now to be let.

AND WHEREAS a meeting of several Churchwardens and Overseers of the poor of several Parrishes within the said Hundreds is intended to be held on monday the 2nd day of June next at Helstone aforesaid in order to consider of the same.

NOW We the major part of the Principal Inhabitants of this Parrish in Vestry assembled for that purpose (usual notice thereof having been given) DO hereby authorize, impower and direct Roger Collins and Thomas Hill Churchwardens and Nicholas Carnbellack and Richard Barkla Overseers of the poor of this parrish or any one or more of

them to attend and be at Helstone at the said time and place and then and there to act, consent, sign and agree in consort with such Churchwardens and Overseers as he or they shall then and there meet to all such matters and things as he or they shall think proper and beneficial for this parrish.

GIVEN under our hands this 27th May 1755. J. Hill, Wm Robinson, Thos Jordan, John Pearce, Joseph Reed, the sign of Peter P. Perry, Roger Jordan, John Pearce, Joseph Reed, the sign of Peter P. Perry, Roger Collins, Thos Hill, the sign of Nicholas N. Carnbellack, Richard Barkla.

The overseers of the poor were first appointed in Queen Elizabeth I's reign, when, the monasteries having been dissolved, the State began to attempt to deal systematically with the question of poor relief. An Act of Parliament was passed in 1572 ordering rates to be levied in every parish to provide funds for relieving the destitute poor, and overseers were everywhere appointed to raise and administer them. The churchwardens were overseers ex-officio, and additional overseers were appointed each year. The new Helston Union took over from the Alms Houses which were maintained, as in every parish, by a rate levied on parishioners. (Wendron Alms Houses were in a field on the site of the present-day turning to Coverack Bridges – to this day still called Alms House Field.). A Union Building in Helston was first sited in Wendron Street in 1755, and when the inmates and staff transferred to the Meneage Street building, it became the Wesleyan Day School.

Above: *Nursing staff of the Poor Law Institution, 1920s. Mrs Perring, the matron, is in the centre of the group.*
Below: *Board of Guardians, 1930. Members were drawn from all of the contributing parishes. The Perrings are to the left at the front. In the centre of the back row is Walter Eva of Manaccan parish.*

When I was at school, there were at least 20 children in the orphanage section of the Union, most of whom went to the Wesleyan Day School with the remainder attending Church Hill School. On their way to lessons they always walked down the street hand in hand, the girls wearing white pinafores and the boys hob-nailed boots, with their hair clipped up in what we used to call the County Council haircut. This particular effect was achieved by Barber Cooke who we used to think must have placed a basin on each head and cut around it. When the orphans went indoors after school they were never allowed out to play and their entire childhood was encircled by that building; it must have been a far from pleasant place for young people to grow up.

The Board of Guardians monitored the Workhouse and controlled the finances. In 1928 when Walter Eva became the Kerrier Rural District Councillor for Manaccan, council meetings were held on Saturday afternoons in the boardroom there. Walter was also a member of the Board of Guardians who met on Saturdays to monitor the work of the relieving officers and to interview some of the clients for poor relief.

When I was a boy Mr and Mrs Perring, my brother John's in-laws, were Master and Matron. There were also several nurses who lived in the three-storey nurses' home at the back of the main building. This was taken down c.1980.

ABOVE THE INFORMATION CENTRE

Opposite Trengrouse Way is the present-day Information Centre where Mr Frank Pill used to live and from where he conducted all of his business as the agent for Redruth Brewery – which served, among others, the Prince's Arms and Globe Hotel. Mr Pill had a big yard (now part of Helston Garages) in which he had a garage where he stored his rarely used car. Before Mr Pill's time in the lovely cottage, the inhabitant was one Mr Orchard, listed in the 1891 census as a malt and brewer's agent.

Next to Mr Pill was a little cottage with a bay window where Mr Jory the mason lived with one of his sisters, Emily. Another sister married William Trengrouse, also a mason. There was an opening down to the back, leading to two cottages where a Mr Cheffers (yet another mason) lived. Next door to this was a Mrs Trevenna. Out on the road was the entrance to Jory's Garage (Willy Jory used to live in Meneage Road), a narrow but deep building which ran down to fields below. Next door was Hayne's Garage, which housed the Cornwall Motor Transport (C.M.T.) buses. Mr Hayne also had petrol pumps there and his sister and her two daughters ran the neighbouring Haynes' Ironmongers. One of the granddaughters, Sheila Tracey, worked as an announcer for the BBC for the news programme *Spotlight*. In May 1960 the old garages were bought by Stanley Carr who started an Austin agency the following year. All of the buildings were later knocked down to make way for what is now Helston Garages, managed by David Carr.

Beyond yet another alleyway was a little sweet shop kept by two spinster sisters by the name of Phillips. Their brother was a recluse and rumour had it that he was a deserter from the First World War. We spent many a penny up there on sweets, entering the shop as quietly as possible, hoping to see him, but try as we might we never did. In the mid 1930s the shop was taken over by a Miss Kneebone.

Next door was a little cottage where Mr Colman the carpenter lived with his son Claud, who, for many years, was the manager of the Star Tea Company. The neighbouring building is now a Peugeot sales room which, during my childhood housed the Post Office's horse-drawn vans (the horses for which were stabled around the back). In the 1881 census, the site where the vehicles were kept was occupied by cottages in which several families lived.

John Toy's Foundry was immediately adjacent and later, when the horses and waggonettes moved out, he turned the building into a plumbing business employing over 20 men. The works were sited at the rear with the horses being shod alongside. The building facing the road was a showroom for the cast-iron items, many of them made by John Toy which are still found in the vicinity today. He was most famous for casting old Cornish ranges similar to those in the museum and many of his farm implements and signposts can still be seen around the countryside. The coal to fire the furnace came into Gweek by boat and was then transported to Meneage Street by horse and cart. As a boy, it was great fun to go up after school on Fridays when they were casting and see the white-hot molten metal with sparks flying everywhere. I remember it running down little channels into the moulds which were bedded down in sand as they cast the fronts and tops of ovens, gate hinges, and so on. John Toy himself lived next to his showroom with a housekeeper but apparently never married.

Top: *Helston Town Band marching down Meneage Street with Jory's and Haynes' Garages side by side in the background, c.1925.*

Above: *Laying pipes for the sewerage scheme, 1921. The two cottages on the right hand side were knocked down in 1951 to make the entrance to Grange Road. Note the telegraph poles on the left hand side and the traffic jam of motorised vehicles even in 1921.*

Upper Meneage Street

Above: Four of a row of five cottages which were demolished to make way for a fruit shop and launderette. The fifth cottage, No. 122, is still lived in.

Right: These two houses were later demolished to allow for road access to the new development of Clies Court.

Left: In the house on the left lived Mr Bolitho, the ex-gold-miner and on the right lived Mr Stephens the tailor.

Right: The Clies. A view of some of the cottages which at one time housed many of the poorer people of the town. These have now been renovated as business premises and a children's play centre.

Upper Meneage Street

Left: *New houses at Clies Court which were built in 1998 to provide sheltered housing.*

Right: *The home of Henry Trengrouse, the inventor of the life-saving rocket apparatus. He lived here with his wife and daughter Mary towards the end of his life, having spent much money on his invention with little recognition or reward.*

Left: *Mr and Mrs Douglas Wearne lived in the bungalow which was formerly the site of his grandparents' home.*

Right: *St Michael's Terrace, a very attractive row of houses at the end of Meneage Street, built before the First World War.*

The white house is where Johnny Chapel had his Tripe Shop. The alley on the right leads to Clies Court.

Modernised Clies Court with its Children's Centre and offices.

The building which is now Hutchinson's Fish and Chip Shop was originally built in the 1930s as a showroom for Toy's Foundry by Mr James Luke, a blacksmith and engineer from St Ives. Afterwards Mr Freeman from Mawgan used it to sell farming equipment and feed before Walter Johns converted it into a café.

Next along the road was Taylor's Tyre Depot which used to be the Trengrouse Stores where William Trengrouse, grandson of the inventor Henry Trengrouse, kept a large premises for selling corn and farming supplies. There was also a covered drive here for loading and unloading and a hoist for raising sacks of corn to the upper storey. Next door there was a row of several cottages, where Mrs Moyle lived, with an opening down to two more houses. The names of the families living there included Pascoe, McCarthy, Williams, Bassett (Eddie), Walters, Chenoweth, Heath and Crowle. In 1950 this row of cottages was knocked down to make way for Grange Road, leading to the new Grange Road Housing Estate built to house Naval personnel transferred from Gosport to RNAS Culdrose.

Back across the road is No. 92, characterised by its tiny panes of glass, and originally Johnny Chapel's Tripe Shop. Johnny's mother, née Lenderyou, was either a farmer or a butcher. There used to be a little entrance here up to Clies Yard with a terrace of houses that had a very high wall at the rear where for a time many of the down-and-outs lived. Although modernised, the area is still pleasant. In the big house next to Johnny Chapel's Tripe Shop lived Tom Pollard, and before that a Miss Woolcocks. Then there was the Blee family, and the Gills, and next up the house in which I was born – 98 Meneage Street – reached by a passageway next door to the surgery. Before the surgery was built, there were three little cottages which housed the Coombes family, Symonds' family and the Reals.

Mr Bolitho, an ex-gold-miner, owned two neighbouring houses, 106 and 108. He and his wife lived in 106 and William Henry Stephens was tenant of 108. A tailor, he did work for Reed and Roberts, Courtney Hocking in Wendron Street and B. Thomas in Meneage Street. As a young man he was a well-known football referee. Later in life he continued his tailoring trade from home.

Up from the surgery is the entrance to the old Clies Yard, where the Luggs had a wheelwright shop and Mr Oates had a smithy. There were also various sheds where people kept their traps, as well as three houses; the Bassetts lived in one (Miss Bassett and her brother) and the Bray family lived in Rose Cottage. These two houses are still standing, but the third house, once home to the Curnows, has long since been knocked down. Next there was a little row of five cottages, the end one of which is still standing. Mr and Mrs Kempthorne, Mr and Mrs Lang, Mr and Mrs Jennings and Mr and Mrs Bob Thomas lived in these cottages and in the one remaining cottage lived a Miss Gill who was a clerk to Helston Garages. Two shops now occupy the site of the four demolished cottages, one being the launderette. Next up from No. 122 is a house set back from the road, once owned by Henry Trengrouse, and where the Tripp family lived with a man called Horatio Richards who kept a hardware shop up the top of Wendron Street. Mr Tripp was an accountant and had three daughters.

Three generations of Brays at Rose Cottage: Granny Bray, daughter Mrs Hooper and grandchild Joan, 1930s.

In the next three terraced houses lived Clifford Bray (No. 124), Miss Becky Bennett (No. 126) and Mr Lugg (No. 128) A little bungalow was built directly opposite the chapel on land which used to belong to Wearnes' the bakers. Before the entrance to the allotments there are also three other little cottages – once occupied by Reggie Curtis and the Bassett and English families.

The building across the street, now housing the squash courts, was originally the Bible Christian Chapel which opened in October 1858. When it closed in the 1960s it was bought by Mr David Carr's father who converted it into a funeral parlour. After that it became a glass warehouse before conversion to squash courts. Next door is a lane which we always knew as Bowden's Lane. Now, however, the old name of Prospect Place has been re-instated. This was the boundary between Helston Borough and Wendron Parish, and an old boundary stone can be seen at its entrance. The area between Prospect Place and what is now Bullock's Lane was called Gweal an Gears (Gweal meaning fields and Gears meaning an Army camp) – the site of an ancient fort overlooking the town. On the south side of Prospect Place, where J.C. Williams now have their undertakers and Chapel of Rest, was, in the 1930s, where Mr W.J. Trezise and his son operated a very fine carpentry business.

Meneage Street, c.1900.

Meneage Street, 2000.

Furry Way

To the left of the present-day Spar shop is Furry Way. At its entrance, and at a right angle to Meneage Street, there were once four cottages called Martin's Row and a joinery workshop belonging to the Martin brothers (carpenters and undertakers) – all of which were demolished to make the road entrance wider. On the south side of Furry Way is Bullock Lane leading to Jubilee Terrace (named after King George V's silver jubilee) and Coronation Place. On the corner of Furry Way and Meneage Street there was a little sweet and groceries shop which later became the Spar. This business was kept by Mrs Richards (a cousin to my mother) who remarried and became Mrs Van Duren.

Almost opposite Furry Way is Oliver's Terrace, and a shop where Mrs Susie Thomas sold groceries. There was also once a row of cottages leading up to the King George V playing field, where the occupants were the Trethowan family, Irwin Thomas' family, the Nicholls family, Tommy Williams and the Blatchfords. Up towards the playing field is St Michael's Terrace where the Misses Carrie and Maud Richards lived in a house with a tennis court at the back. As well as doing a lot of work for the hospital, they were also connected with the church for which they formed their own tennis club, and in addition they ran the Flora Day Ball at Godolphin Hall. Also living in the terrace were Mr Faull the blacksmith, Felix Williams, Gordon Pearce and Mr Mac Trezise, one-time Mayor of Helston who had an undertaker's in Bowden's Lane and who did much for local charity.

Whitewash Wall opposite the entrance to Furry Way is well known to pedestrians of Meneage Street and is still as white as it has always been. It is at this point that Meneage Street becomes Meneage Road, although when I was growing up, Meneage Road – from Whitewash Wall to the Cottage Hospital – was always known as Lizard Road. In one of the houses up on the wall lived a man called Josiah Ould. A gardener for Sir Montague Rogers, he was a self-taught, learned character who enjoyed great respect in the town and became a J.P. (Justice of the Peace) and Town Councillor. He never uttered a word that was not well considered. The last house on Whitewash Wall was home to Gerry Rodda who worked in James' furnishing shop and was Ambulance Superintendent.

Top: *Opposite the Whitewash Wall was Bullock Lane (perhaps once Bulwarks Lane). Drovers brought cattle from the Lizard Peninsula to Helston at the start of the weekend and rested them off Meneage (Lizard) Road. On Mondays they were taken along the lane to the Castle Green market. The road existed long before the market.*
Above: *Harvesting in the fields behind St Michael's Terrace. Much of the land east of Meneage Street and Meneage Road was laid down to open, farmed fields. Here workers pose in an area now covered by houses.*

WHITEHILL

From Bullock Lane up to well beyond the cemetery (and incorporating Meneage Road) was an area known as Whitehill (probably because of the silver mine there). Up on the bank is another row of cottages which includes Lynvale Guest House, a property always known as the 'Bank'. The two large houses that stand on their own to the south of the Bank were built by Mr Joe White who, in his retirement, had a taxi which he kept in Cade's Yard. A letter from his daughter, Mrs M. Burge, written on 1 June 1996, includes the following:

My Father was Joseph Trenary White; he lived in one of the two houses which he built in 1897 in Meneage Road, next to the little All Saints Church near the cemetery. My brother was born in 1902 and I in 1906. I was known as May White and worked in the General Post Office in Meneage Street. I was sent to Truro every day for six months by train and qualified in morse code, because that was the way telegrams were sent and received. I was then a telegraphist on the staff.

My father was a builder and undertaker and built the shop and premises in Meneage Street which was Hawke's the photographers, and also built the shop next to the Wesleyan chapel in Coinagehall Street; it was a butcher's shop I remember. Father was the third person in Helston to have a car, the first being Mr H.A.L. Rowe with his dark red 6h.p. Tonneau AF 60, the registration documents and licence of which are in the museum, and the second being Henry Toy, manager of Barclay's Bank, who became Sir Henry Toy. I went to the County School in Wendron Street which my father had to pay fees for in those days.

All Saints Church was built in the early part of the 19th century to serve the southern side of town and remained in use until the late 1970s. The adjacent cemetery and Mortuary Chapel were opened at about the same time. Following closure of the church, the Parochial Church Council made it the object of a community programme, and in 1984 work began on the near derelict building, restoring and converting it into a resource and skills centre to meet the needs of the town and Lizard area.

Right: *Chapel of Rest, Helston Cemetery.*

Below: *The pair of houses at Whitehill built by Mr Joe White, father of Mrs M. Burge of Penarth.*

Above: *All Saints Church, built in the early-19th century.*

Helston Cottage Hospital, 1924, built as a memorial to the men who lost their lives in the First World War. Many Helston men returned from the war with only one leg or having been badly affected by gas. The Cottage Hospital was officially opened in 1923 by William James Johns, Mayor of Helston. It was designed to look more like a home than a hospital.

MENEAGE (LIZARD) ROAD

On the east side of the road above the Whitewash Wall are a number of cottages which have remained largely unchanged. The only feature of this landscape that has disappeared is a little smallholding kept by the Bassett family at the end of the buildings. John Kemp Bray's family lived opposite the cemetery and had a shop there where they sold camping equipment. The owners of much property in Meneage Road, they also had two tennis courts which Church Street Chapel used to use for their club. Dennis Bray, one-time Mayor of Camborne, was the 12th child and youngest son of this family. The eldest son was killed in France on 3 September 1918, just three months before Dennis was born.

James Henry Thomas continued his father's business in Meneage Road, at first as a wheelwright and later repairing carriages and woodwork on vans, as well as assembling bodies on lorry chassis. Outside was a smithy run by Mr Faull and a sawpit where Mr Mitchell worked cutting planks for lorry beds. Christopher's lorries were all planked out there and J. Henry Thomas used to paint them and put on the signwriting. It was a busy little place.

Next to the smithy was a house occupied by Mr and Mrs Bassett with two semi-detached houses beyond them; the first occupied by Mrs Crapp and her daughter, the second by Mrs Crowle and her two girls Kathleen (Kay) and Thelma. Then there was the house which the Lukes built, followed by a smallholding run by Mr Julian who was also Town Crier. His neighbours on the other side were the Bassetts and the Broadhursts. Next along was the little bungalow of Charlie Bassett. During his time as Mayor, Mr William Johns, the bank manager, also lived nearby in a large house. Charlie Oliver, the butcher, lived up there also and had a small slaughter house at the back of his dwelling. Next door to this is the last of the big houses before the children's home, Trevenen House. It was once home to William Trengrouse who married Miss Jory.

To the west of Meneage Road and next to the cemetery was the show field where yearly shows and even, on one occasion, the Royal Cornwall Show, were held. During the Second World War it housed a prisoner of war camp and is now being developed for high-quality housing. Nansloe Lodge protected the road down to Nansloe Manor, the home of Sir Montague Rogers, a solicitor and mining agent.

Further along Meneage Road stands Helston Community Hospital. The original hospital was funded by donations as a memorial to those who lost their lives in the First World War and the foundation stones were laid on 19 May 1922, a year before its official opening in 1923, when it became known as the Cottage Hospital.

Top: *Trevenen House and the charity lands, landscaped and planted with ornamental shrubs and sections of Cornish granite.*
Centre and above: *Old Children's Home at the top of Meneage Road and a Christmas party for the children put on by the Girl's League in 1948.*

I remember when they were building the Cottage Hospital in the early 1920s and I went up there to see Great Uncle Dick Tavener (born in 1854) who was digging out the foundations by hand – by then he was well into his sixties. He had come to Helston in the late-19th century to work on the laying of the railway line from Gwinear Road to Helston and when this was finished went to the Scilly Isles to help build a fort. He took with him his wife and my mother's sister, Aunt Katie, who lived with them. He later returned to Helston to help dig out the Coronation Lake at the bottom of town just before the First World War. Winns did the building of the hospital and my Uncle Ernie made all of the windows in the workshop at St Johns.

The land across the road from the hospital (since developed with modern bungalows) was set aside for allotments, one of which my father had. Most families had one in my childhood days and we could see them all laid out along Clodgey Lane and also opposite the Mormon church. At the top of the road is what used to be the Children's Home built by Cornwall County Council whilst Sir Henry Toy was Chairman. It was built as two houses to make it much more of a home than an institution. The building has now been separated into two private houses. Turning left into Clodgey Lane at the top of Meneage Road, one comes to the house (a former farm) on the right, which has always been known as Casterills. Despite many enquiries the meaning of the name has not been discovered although Revd Canon Doble mentions it in his book, *Two Cornish Parishes in the Eighteenth Century* in connection with 'Goon' in 1754 (Goon meaning downs). As there is a huge well at Casterhills, clearly intended to water a large number of people, it could be that the word refers to a building of some kind, perhaps even a monastic gathering place.

Helston Downs

To the right of the top of Meneage Road is Captain's Lane – originally the main road across Helston Downs to St Keverne and the Lizard. On the right of this stands a blocked-up gateway, formerly the pedestrian entrance to Helston Downs playing field. Almost opposite the turning to Culdrose Manor was a stone which marked a mile's distance from the town clock; any races run in the town would be between these two points. The old cycle track was just over the hedge and also on the Downs were a football pitch and a cricket pitch. Iron railings separated the two, with kissing gates to allow access into the cricket field and pavilion. To the right of the main road, beyond the pedestrian access gate, there was a second gateway designed to allow the horse and roller through. There was also a pathway across the field which lead down to Eglos Dairy Farm, where one could turn right to take a path to the Gunwalloe Road by way of Content. The main road across the Downs went straight out to White House where there was a 'Y' junction with turnings down Rose Hill to St Keverne and the Lizard. There was once a farm there called Killecanchor where Kenny Thomas and his sister lived.

Listening to records on the gramaphone in front of J.H. Thomas' Coach Works in Meneage Road. Left to right: Nicholls Williams, Bill Angove, Leslie Ould.

The playing area was regularly used by the fire brigade for drill and also served as a starting point for many parades through the town. On 9 December 1942, the Colours of the 1st Battalion, the Duke of Cornwall's Light Infantry, were here transferred to the 6th Battalion DCLI. At the outbreak of war the 1st Battalion was in India and moved to Iraq to join the 10th Indian Division in 1941. During the following spring they motored from Iraq to Tobruk in the Western Desert and immediately on arrival were sent into the 'Cauldron' battle area south west of Tobruk. There at Bir-el-Harmat on 5 and 6 June 1942, in hastily prepared defensive positions, they met the full force of Rommel's armour and lost nearly all of their men. In November of that year 12 survivors joined the 6th Battalion DCLI at Helston in a ceremony renaming it the 1st DCLI. The 1st Battalion Colours were received by Lt Colonel G.J. Fletcher, Commanding Officer of the 6th Bn DCLI, from the 1st Bn Colour Party, and the ceremony was concluded with a march past at the Helston AFC ground (*see page 14*).

In February 1944 Helston Borough Council received notice from the Admiralty that Helston Downs was to be part of the land required for the building of RNAS Culdrose, heralding a major change for Helston's economy and demography.

Chapter 3: Helston, The Town of My Youth 1920–39

Wendron Street

As its name suggests this is the street which leads to Wendron. On the north side the first shop, which is now closing, is where Mr Barnett ran his business for many decades. In the late 1930s, Miss Cossentine ran her private school in the rooms above the shop. Next door are the solicitors Randle Thomas & Thomas in the former home of the Cotton family who ran an outfitting department on one side of the road and a drapers on the other. On the ground either side of the front door of the solicitors there is a concrete plat; each side was originally surrounded by rails with steps leading down to the kitchens and on the other side was the tradesman's entrance. Before Mr Cotton bought it, the entire property was the Globe Hotel, which in 1880 was run by the Ellis family. Mr Bassett, who had the tobacconists higher up the street, once told me that he remembered the carriages coming down from the station and stopping outside the front entrance to allow visitors to go up the steps into the hotel. Leading from the entrance side of the hotel there was a tunnel which went under the street to the other side of the hotel, enabling guests to avoid crossing the street.

Next to Randle Thomas & Thomas was a grocers owned by Harry Jory, the brother of Willie who ran the garage in Meneage Street and acted as chief of the fire brigade. His neighbour was Peter Sandry the hairdresser, a great story teller who broadcast for the BBC many times with great success, despite the fact that listeners could not enjoy the wonderful facial expressions with which he used to amuse his audience. He had a great repertoire of local dialect and could reproduce all of the variations peculiar to the speech within the local parishes. He was endowed with a cheery good-heartedness which, together with his talent for story telling and dressing up, made him a popular choice for entertainments in local villages and neighbouring towns. In this way he helped to raise hundreds of pounds for charities, churches and chapels and various other organisations. He was also the regular Father Christmas at Sir Courtenay Vyvyan's Childrens' Christmas Party for the children of St Martin and Mawgan (see *Around Helston in the Old Days* by A.S. Oates). Next door at 8 Wendron Street was the print shop John Lander & Sons (cousins of my mother).

Across the street, next to the Globe Hotel, was the back entrance to the Post Office. The main office faced into Meneage Street but all post came out through that back door and on to the mail carts lined up waiting at the back gate. Beyond this busy entrance was the Globe Tap.

Inez Trenerry, hairdresser of Wendron Street and keen motor enthusiast with her Austin 7.

Part of Redruth Brewery, it sold beer across one long bar. Next door was a fruit and sweet shop kept by the Misses Oates, sisters of Mr Henry Oates who went to London and became a director of Cook & Son Company of 22 St Paul's Churchyard. They also had another sister, Mrs Diamond, who lived in Godolphin Road.

Next door was the tobacconist, Arthur Basset, who came down from Bude to set up business in Helston. During and after the First World War smoking became very popular and tobacconists nationwide thrived. Next door was the Misses Symons' boot and shoe shop, formerly a pub. Their neighbour was Mr Smith with his fruit and grocery business who at Christmas time ran a bazaar at the Star Hotel where he rented the Long Room in which to display his festive goods.

In the next shop the Wills family sold home-made cakes and buns, and above this was the cinema, built as a Baptist chapel in the 1830s. For several years it showed nothing but silent films and it then closed down to be taken on by John James who used it to house a furniture shop and store. Later it reverted to a cinema showing 'talkies' and was run by a Mr Hill.

On the other side of the street was Mr Hawke's butchers. He had two sons, Harry and Leslie. Harry died from wounds received during the First World War and Leslie suffered mustard-gas poisoning which affected his speech badly, but he managed to carry on the butchering business. His daughter Phyllis moved to South Africa and I visited her when I had the good fortune to go to Durban in 1996.

Wendron Street

Above: *The entrance to the old Grammar School.*

Top right: *Bassett's Gift Shop. The small shop in the centre of the picture is where Arthur Bassett started his tobacconists shop, with Miss Symon's shoe shop above it. When she retired the Bassetts took over her shop and her house. Eileen Bassett, the daughter, married Perry Roberts and they lived in the house on the right of the picture.*

Right: *Godolphin Hall built in 1834.*

Below: *The solicitors occupy the first house on the left, followed by Harry Jory's grocers, Peter Sandry the barber and Landers the printers.*

Above: *Pascoe's dilapidated monumental masons shop which was demolished and replaced by flats and a pathway leading up to the housing estate and car park.*

On the other side of Hawke's butchers was Gordon Lory's cycle store, where his mother ran the shop at the front while Gordon maintained motorcycles in the workshop at the rear. Always outside the door was a parrot tethered to a perch and this bird's language often left much to be desired. Mrs Lory sold all sorts of goods for bicycles, from pumps to carbide to run the lamps. (The carbide lamp, also used on cars in the very early days, was a three-part construction comprising the headpiece with the burner and reflector, the middle piece in the shape of a cylinder which held water, and the bottom piece – also cylindrical – which held carbide. These sections were all screwed together and on the top of the water cylinder was a turn tap which controlled the drip rate of the water on to the carbide. As the acetylene gas was generated it would come out of the burner allowing one to light it with a match. The lamps were not very effective and although people might just make one out coming along the road, there was little chance of seeing one's way by the light they gave out.).

Next along the street was Godolphin Hall, a large Gothic building which, like many of the key buildings in Helston, was constructed in the 1830s. It incorporated a reading room, a billiard and snooker room, the Odd Fellow's Hall, and upstairs a big room where dances and concerts were held, as were Reed John's monthly sales of household furniture. The old caretaker, Jim Hellier, lived in a flat upstairs. In the mid 1920s on every Flora Day there would be a grand ball in the evening, organised by Misses Carrie and Maud Richards who were great characters in the town, and all the participants of the midday dance would come to dance again. Until the 1920s, the midday dance used to end with a form of square dance called the Roger de Coverly, followed by the National Anthem. Alongside the Godolphin Club is the old Grammar School entrance with its 19th-century Tudor doorway and mouldings. Once known as the 'Little Eton of England' it had several distinguished students, including Charles Kingsley and Henry Irvine (then living with his grandparents in Penzance and known as 'Broadrib').

Where the car park is now there was an old thatched house, the residence of Mr Oates Eva, an important Helston builder and one-time Borough Surveyor. This was where my uncle, Fred James, served his apprenticeship. The builder's yard was behind the house. This was followed by a row of thatched cottages behind which were courts containing more thatched cottages and quite a collection of people. Many members of my mother's family, the Jameses, were born here – at what was then known as No. 43 Wendron Street.

Across the road on the south side of the street was a Mr Colenzo and his wife, a lovely couple who used to sell ice cream and sweets in their front room parlour. The house next door with the bay window was home to Mr Jeffrey the coalman, a keen member of the band and one who appears in many Flora Day photographs over the years.

On the site of the development of flats and the steps leading up towards Parc-an-Dower, there was a monumental masons run by a Mr Phillip Spargo and later by the Pascoe brothers. In due course, it was torn down, together with Mr Jeffrey's house below, to provide the site for a new block of flats. In the adjoining building (with bay windows on either side of the door) lived Mr and Mrs Courtney Hocking – he a tailor and she a very good singer. The couple had one son.

I do not recall who lived in the little cottages next door, but there were steps which lead to a cobbled opening at the back of which was the Salvation Army Hall. A once popular organisation in Helston, the Salvation Army had its own band and a large following. Mr Edwin Upex was one of the first officers to come to Helston and he later set up a boot and shoe shop which eventually became Upex's Garage.

The big house with the bay windows opposite the ambulance station housed the telephone exchange. As one entered the front door the exchange was on the left hand side. There was only one room in which six or eight ladies operated manual machines. With improving technology and greater demand for phones, they were moved to the new Post Office in Coinagehall Street.

Helston Salvation Army, c1924.

*Helston Salvation Army Band, c.1935.
Left to right, back: Vernie Wear, Captain Griggs, Garfield Jackson, Lt Black, Sidney Reynolds; front: Jack Pascoe, Nelson Pascoe, Bill Philpott, Maurice Kempthorne, Willie Wear.*

The house where Bob Fitzsimmons was born.

St John's Ambulance

When I joined the ambulance at the age of 12, I was working at Pascoe's Shoe Shop where another employee, Tommy Dunstan, persuaded me to join the cadets. These started in 1928, four years after the opening of the ambulance station in Wendron Street (which before this date was stationed at Jory's Garage in Meneage Street). I was only the second member to join them, the first being Clarence Ould, and I enjoyed myself immensely, staying with them until I went to London in 1934. When I left they gave me an engraved, silver cigarette case which I kept with me for most of the war only to have it stolen in a cinema in Cairo!

After lectures we were tested by a Dr Blackwood from Redruth (another man with a wooden leg), who on one occasion asked a boy named Kendall what he would do if he arrived home to find a dog attacking his sister. Kendall answered: 'I haven't got a sister, sir', to which Dr Blackwood replied 'Supposing the dog was savaging your mother then?' 'We haven't got a dog, sir' came Kendall's retort and so it went on until Dr Blackwood finally got the better of him.

Top: *Statue of Bob Fitzsimmons in Timaru, New Zealand.*

Above: *The station which opened in 1924. Miss Cox's private school was run in the house below.*

Upper Wendron Street

A part of the building which now houses the motor parts shop was used by two ex-Navy brothers called Polglaze who made ornaments out of serpentine stone. Next door to that was Upex's Garage, previously a shop run by Horatio Richards who sold paraffin, candles, brushes and brooms, etc.

His neighbour further up the street was the head cashier of the bank, and two doors up from there is the lovely 17th-century thatched cottage – birthplace of the famous boxer Bob (Ruby Robert) Fitzsimmons (although some elderly people claim that he was not born here at all, but near the bottom of town). The plaque over the door recounts how, in 1887, at the age of 34, Fitzsimmons knocked out Gentleman Jim Corbett at Carson City, U.S.A. to become heavyweight champion of the world. Also middleweight and light-heavyweight champion, Fitzsimmons was the first man to become a triple title holder. When the family went to Timaru, South Island, New Zealand, one brother remained at home and married into the Lander family. On 5 September 1987, in the city of Timaru, the Prime Minister of New Zealand, the Right Honourable David Lange, formally unveiled a life-size statue of Bob Fitzsimmons, sculpted by Margaret Windhausen van den Burgh.

To the rear of these houses there are two more little cottages which backed on to the old Wesley School playground which later became the site of a bungalow (*top*). As children we used to go up a flight of steps at street level on to the playground, with the boys' toilets on the right hand side, and up a second flight of steps to a level piece of ground on which the school was built. This was 'F' shaped, with the central bar of the 'F' being the wash-rooms, divided down the centre with boys on one side and girls on the other. There was barely room for all of the children who attended the school but, being an old granite workhouse building, this made it no less forbidding.

Dog racing at Beacon Barns Field, mid 1920s.

Fire Ambulance and crew, 1924.
Left to right: H. Mitchell, R.G. Rows, F. Woolacott, Supt J.B. Gilbert, G.R. Rodda, T. Dunstan, G.H. Rich.

Penrose Road

Immediately opposite the Fitzsimmons' house is Penrose Road, which was always known as 'New Road', despite having been built in the 1830s. It is dominated by the former County School, which backs on to the Godolphin Hall in Wendron Street. The pupil-teacher centre of Penrose Road and Wendron Street opened in 1905 admitting 120 boys and girls. It was built close to the site of the old Grammar School (which opened in 1834 after moving from its site of 1610) and attached to the original Passmore Edwards Technical Institute and School of Art, erected in 1897 at the personal expense of J. Passmore Edwards. Comprising a chemical laboratory, classrooms and offices, the centre was headed, in 1910, by Mr Hayden.

In 1840 the newly-built United Methodist Church was opened on the corner of Penrose Road and Church Street on the site of the brewery which once stood there. The building, with seating for around 600, cost £4000 and had a very good organ, presented by Mr J. Rogers Pascoe. Unfortunately, the foundations were built on the old brewery workings and eventually began to give way. In 1960 the chapel, in which I had spent many happy days, was demolished.

Shute Hill

On the side of the old Wesley School is Shute Hill, a steep slope with a handrail running up the centre. On the right hand side is the water shute after which the hill is named and where pigs were once killed and the carcasses washed. Mr Peter James lived in the house at the bottom on the left and had his carpentry workshop to the rear, with stables and a storage shed for the town's hearse below. He also owned the fields at the top of Shute Hill. On the right of the hill is the old prison, built in 1837 with cells and exercise yard – a much-needed facility in the town at that time because of the brawls among miners that ensued after heavy drinking bouts. It was built at a cost of £730, and provided sections for both male and female prisoners. In 1853, it was run by an Irishman, James Fitzsimmons, the father of the famous boxer.

Next door to the prison was a gate leading to a field in which greyhound racing was organised by Mr Edwin James the baker. The dummy hare was attached via a rope to the back wheel of an upside-down bicycle, and pulled across a straight stretch of field, 100 yards long, with the greyhounds in hot pursuit. On the left of the field was a stile to a footpath leading to Clodgey Lane.

Top left: *This bungalow with the garage beneath stands on the site where the town's hearse was kept by Peter James, who also had a workshop here.*

Above: *Harvesting in Beacon Barns Field.*

Left and inset: *The Old Prison, built in 1836, where Bob Fitzsimmons' father was jailer.*

Middle part of Godolphin Road, c.1903. Lugg's Temperance Hotel is on the left. The white building on the right was a private school. Note the unmade road and the kennel.

Upper Godolphin Road, 1910, with the newly-built Police Station on the right and the house with the display boards on the left which was later the home of Fred James, Reg's uncle.

Godolphin Road

Godolphin Road takes its name from Lord Godolphin, a generous patron of the borough, who owned vast areas of land in and around Helston. Sidney, the first Lord Godolphin, was Lord High Treasurer of England, and his son married Henrietta Churchill, the eldest daughter of his great friend the Duke of Marlborough. Later there was no Godolphin male heir, and the property and interests passed to Francis Godolphin Osborne, the 5th Duke of Leeds and son of Mary Godolphin.

The road is the continuation of Wendron Street and starts at Penrose Road. The first two villas up from Penrose Road are numbered as 'Godolphin Road', but the four houses following (opposite the old school) are named 'Kroonstadt Villas'. They were built in 1902 by a man who made his fortune gold mining in South Africa (Kroonstadt being a South-African mine).

On the same side of the road was a small set of cottages where the Prisks lived – descendants of whom once kept the Horse and Jockey Hotel in Meneage Street. Before one arrives at what used to be Lugg's Temperance Hotel, there is a little alleyway known as Factory Yard. I was told that this was where fat and tallow were melted down to make candles, but I have been unable to confirm the story. Helston was full of characters and one such lived here; Tommy Lugg – who was 'ten short of a dozen' – toured the houses every Friday night, knocking on the doors of his 'customers' to enquire whether the occupant wanted any tea, coffee or cocoa. He would knock on my mother's door and she would ask for a quarter of tea. Tommy always gave the same reply: 'I've just sold out, but I will bring that around to you next week.' This went on week after week. If asked by my mother where he was going, Tommy would often reply with a sullen look, 'I'm going home to put the ducks to roost.'

Across the road there are some very pleasant old houses. One particularly large one was the home of Mr J.B. Martin, the chemist. This was later owned by Mr Sturgess of Ward Cornwall. The three neighbouring houses were where the Methodist ministers lived – a superintendent minister and two subordinates. Side on to the road is the house which was a girls' private school and later the home of Mr Williams the chief cashier at Lloyds Bank. No. 17 Godolphin Road was once just a broken-down cottage but my uncle, Mr Fred James, bought it and rebuilt it, together with a carpenter's workshop and builder's yard to the rear.

On the north side of Godolphin Road lies the entrance to Cades Parc, a modern housing development. All of this property once belonged to the Cade family. Mr Cade was a former Town Registrar and also ran a forage merchants in Cades Yard, Meneage Street. In 1910 Mr Alfred Charles Cade lived in Godolphin Road and his sister, Miss E. Cade, lived in Meneage Street.

Immediately before the police station, built in 1902, was Harvey's Coal Yard, which has now been turned into garages owned by Donald Williams. Once past the police station, one gets a view down on to a new row of houses where there was once a little line of four or five cottages known as Lower Silver Hill (its name deriving from the silver mine there, the adit of which came out on Well Moors). Next along the road is the red-brick building known as Godolphin House, now a retirement home. Alfred Pascoe, who kept the Regent Hotel in Coinagehall Street, used to live there and also kept it as a boarding house. When Alfred died, Mr Sturton, the Excise Officer, moved in. Next to Godolphin House there was a lane which led down to the County Yard, the site of the local road repair offices and where the repair materials were stored. In the large house next door lived the two Miss Julians from Turnpike Farm. One later married Mr Medlyn. Their neighbour was Mr Prisk, the County Surveyor, whose son followed in his father's footsteps and is now living in Truro where he runs Prisk & Co., the house surveyors.

The two pleasant granite houses opposite the Police Station, built in 1903, were occupied by professional and business people. They are followed by a row of eight small cottages and two more large granite houses. In the middle of the cottages there is a little pathway which leads through to Higher Silver Hill and Sanctuary Lane where there was another small sweet shop. The first of the two large granite houses is now the Trelawny Retirement Home, and was the home of Richard Gundry Rapson, J.P., who used to live in the house in Meneage Street which is now the NatWest bank. A later occupant of this house was Mr James Bennet Gilbert who had the newsagents and stationary shop at the bottom of Meneage Street. Next door was 'Lamorna', formerly the Manse for Church Street Chapel. Higher up the road, opposite Station Road, there is another pair of high-class, semi-detached houses. The Registrar, Mr Fred Thomas, lived in one, and Mrs Eddy, a teacher from the Wesley Day School, lived in the other (called 'Brenta Villa').

COURTENAY HOCKING,

Practical Ladies' and Gents' Tailor,
Costumier and Breeches Maker,

Penlee House, Godolphin Road,

HELSTON.

Clericals & Liveries.   Satisfaction Guaranteed.

In the first pair of houses, far left, lived Mrs Eddy, the schoolteacher at the Wesleyan Day School.

The cottages to the right once contained two shops – both general stores run by Mrs Stinchcombe and Mrs Coles. The adjoining pair of granite houses were occupied by Mr J.B. Gilbert who kept the newspaper shop in Meneage Street. Next door to his home was the Manse for the Church Street Methodist Church.

Station Road

On the corner of Station Road is Moses Villas, followed by a row of cottages and a pair of semi-detached houses where the residents were mainly railway workers. Mr E.G. Curtis, who kept the grocers before Trounsons arrived, lived in the last detached, double-fronted house with his daughter, who later married a Methodist minister.

On the site below (since developed with bungalows) there was nothing but church fields and a pathway leading to St Michael's. Between Station Road and the church there was just one house, Tenderah, the home of the Tyack family and subsequently a hotel. Walking through the fields from Station Road brought one to the house of Mr Hayden (the headmaster of the Grammar School) at the bottom of Church Hill. The newer properties in this area included the house of Mr Cunnack and that of Ernest Winn. On the right of Station Road was the station itself and the ramp leading to the platform still remains.

The Helston Railway Act came into being on 9 July 1880 and the railway was officially opened on 8 May 1887. It was a huge success, bringing increased employment and prosperity to the area, conveying local produce to new markets well away from Cornwall and bringing tourists to the Lizard, who began to travel by rail rather than by coach or car. Helston Station was a very busy place, with a huge amount of produce being transported out of Helston, such as cabbages, broccoli, eggs, butter and rabbits.

At Predannack there is an inlet called Soapy Cove, where a soft serpentine stone was extracted for years. All of the buildings have now gone, but the cove workings are still visible. For many years there were thousands of tons of soft serpentine brought to Helston Railway Station and sent by train to be processed. A great deal of stone from the quarry at Porthoustock was also transported by way of Helston Railway. (Some of the serpentine used to build Regent Street shop front was quarried, shaped and polished in Poltesco, floated out on pontoons, then loaded on to barges and later off-loaded on the Thames Reaches.).

Leading up from the railway station, towards the school, is a pathway known as Cinder Path, so called because of the cinders which were taken from the engines, crushed and put down here. Only wide enough for two people, the path leads to the top of Church Hill, and over the years many pupils arriving by bus at the station walked along it to the County School. The houses on the left are all comparatively new and I can remember them being built. This useful little thoroughfare was the property of the railway and was closed for one day every year so as to continue the right of ownership. On the right hand side were the allotments for the use of the railway staff including the Station Master.

Around the corner at the bottom of Station Road and at the end of the rails was the old engine house whilst up the other side of the station, on the left hand side, was the location of Gweek Company's coal business. With the coming of the railway, coal was delivered by train, whilst

Above: *Henshorn Court Community Centre. This was the former goods loading building and the whole complex now offers sheltered accommodation.*

Left: *Railwaymen at Nancegollan Station on the Helston to Gwinear Road line, mid 1930s. Left to right: Bernard Pooley, Terrance Williams, Percy Charles.*

Turnpike House which stood at the junction of the Redruth and Falmouth roads and which was demolished in 1938.

Helston motor cars leaving the railway station for the Lizard and Mullion in the early 1900s.

originally it had came into Gweek by boat and then on to Helston by horse and cart. Harveys of Hayle also had their coal yard near the station.

Above the station on the right was Helston's main slaughterhouse, built between the wars on the fields to the right of the present-day Henshorn Court. The business provided employment for a great many people, and hundreds of cattle, sheep, and pigs were slaughtered there each week (in a far more humane fashion than that used in the old killing houses). A lot of the meat was transported out of Helston on the railway and, there being no refrigeration, the carcasses were put straight into waggons with louvered sides and sent off to the Midlands and London. The hides meanwhile went over to Grampound Road to be cured. Sadly, at the time of writing the Grampound tannery faces closure, having for generations been in the ownership of the Croggons (who still have their own apprentice cordwainers). Grampound leather was said to be the best and the Croggons exported their product all over the world.

Harvey's builders' merchant was a Hayle rather than a Helston firm and they also owned the coal yard at the bottom of town where Medlyn Court Flats now stand. Harveys also had interests in mining engineering and exported mining equipment worldwide.

The original intention was to extend the railway to the Lizard, via Mawgan and Cury, but in 1903 the GWR (Great Western Railway), who by that time owned the track, decided to buy five 22-seater motor vehicles to connect selected stations with outlying districts. The first of these GWR road motors came into service between Helston and the Lizard on 17 August 1903 and the service continued to run until 1933, when it was taken over by the Western National Bus Company. The latter provided a much improved, wider-ranging service which connected towns, villages and hamlets to the nearest railway station.

At the top of Godolphin Road, almost opposite Station Road, lies Sanctuary Lane – once a back entrance to the high-class houses in Godolphin Road. Going towards town on the left hand side were Beacon Barns Fields, followed by the allotments, upon which bungalows were later built. On the right hand side there were five cottages known as Higher Silver Hill, with the footpath leading to Godolphin Road. At the end of the lane was the prison and the top of Shute Hill.

Also at the top of Godolphin Road are two large grey houses, in one of which lived Mr Arthur Bassett the butcher. In the little row of cottages just beyond lived railway workers, such as Charlie Kendall and Dick Williams – and, with the arrival of the buses, the bus workers as well. Winn's Row (also for railway workers and properly called Church Lane) was built by Mr Winn who lived in the corner house looking down Godolphin Road. Mr Sampson (an engine driver) and his wife Mary lived in No. 1 with their two daughters Rene and Olive, later to be replaced by Taffy Legg (a lorry driver) and his wife with their three children. No. 2 was home to Richard and Matilda Bassett, with their sons Richard and Jimmy. The Nancollis family (whose menfolk worked for the railway) lived in No. 3 and were followed by Charlie Pascoe (a lorry driver) and his wife, with son George. After the Pascoes came Fred Rowe, with his wife and daughter Pauline – in turn replaced by Charlie Opie, his wife and their sons Jack and Telfer (who started up Turnpike Garage). My great uncle, Dick Tavener, lived in No. 4 with his wife and he too was initially a railway worker. No. 5 was occupied by Jan Jory, his wife and two sons, Henry (a station worker) and Jan junr. George and Emma Moyle lived in No. 6, with their sons Percy, Reggie, Ernie and Norman.

As well as being home to numerous railway workers and their families, Winn's Row was also part of a footpath leading to St Michael's Church. The path started at Tresprison, skirted Clodgey Lane, led into the top of Godolphin Road, Winn's Row, before leading up Church Lane and down Church Hill to the church itself.

Top: *Engine 4548 at Helston Station. Note the Helston signal box and the group of three 'shunters' talking with the foreman C.P. Carnell.*
Above: *A group at Nancegollan Station. Left to right: Terence Williams, G. Williams, Nelson Cleaves, Bill Angove, Tommy Champion, Telfer Pethick (squatting), Tony Hitchens, ? Williams, Charlie Uren.*

Coinagehall Street

Left: *Next to Woolworths used to be E.C. Oliver's butchers. The opticians next door is Batemans which at one time belonged to David Rae.*

Right: *Roy Doble's jewellers was the Star Tea Company, with William T. Roger's china shop next door.*

Left: *The left-hand-end cottage cottage is now the Lady Street Night Club where Tom Wearne the picture framer once lived.*

Right: *Left to right: Barclays Bank, Reginald Rogers (solicitor), Mr Milne the dentist and the opening to 'Cobbled Ope' leading to Five Wells.*

COINAGEHALL STREET

Left: *The building on the left with the two bay windows is the Job Centre which was at one time the Star Hotel where a large stone in the pavement marks the main entrance to the carriage-way.*

Right: *Kneebone's Cycle Shop with Woolworths alongside, 1968. The whole block is now occupied by the chain.*

Left: *Coinagehall Street, 1971. Note the Star Hotel up for sale, the International Stores and W.T. Rogers.*

Right: *Star Hotel, May 1971. Before the war the 'Long Room' was regularly used at Christmas time for displays of Christmas fare.*

Turnpike and Clodgey Lane

At the junction of the Redruth and Falmouth roads was the Round House, otherwise known as the Toll House, or Turnpike. To the left of this was Turnpike Dairy, which sold milk, butter and eggs. On Turnpike Corner, where Kernow Cars are now, was a farm run by the Julian family. Later the dairy was run by the Thomases. Opposite, in Clodgey Lane, was a big garage which the two Opie brothers, Charlie and Jim, built to house their business. In the 1920s Clodgey Lane was just wide enough for a horse and cart, with passing places, but over the years it has been widened two or three times. In 1943, when RNAS Culdrose was being built, Clodgey Lane carried all of the necessary building materials for the base. These materials were brought by lorry from Nancegollan Station, up Coinagehall Street, straight up Wendron Street, and through a right turn at the turnpike into Clodgey Lane, round to the T junction at the Cottage Hospital and into the base. In the mid 1950s, during the construction of houses for naval personnel, Clodgey Lane was widened and the by-pass opened.

A Walk Around Coinagehall Street

Coinagehall Street gets its name from the former Coinage Hall which stood in the middle of the street until the beginning of the 19th century when it was demolished to widen the road. In 1305 under the Charter of Tinners of Helleston King Edward I made Helston one of the four coinage towns in the West. The tin mined in the area was all brought to Helston in large ingots (of about 3.5 cwt) to be assayed and each ingot was given the stamp of approval with the Duchy Seal which bears the arms of Richard, Earl of Cornwall.

If one begins a tour around the street at the Guildhall and looks down Coinagehall Street one sees the drapers on the right. For many years this was Wakehams the chemists, owned, before Mr Wakeham, by a Devonian, Mr Drew, who lived above the shop at the time of the 1881 census. Mr Wakeham extended the shop and also ran the old stamp office. He had two sons, Norton and Fred, a Wing Commander in the RAF whom I chanced to meet once in Egypt. There was also a daughter called Phyllis, who was the life and soul of the party and who was Mayoress once when Bill Scott (a widower) was Mayor. All the Wakehams were very nice people and they lived in Leslie House at the bottom of Lady Street. Later in life Miss Wakeham became a very active member of the Royal British Legion (Women's Section).

The shop below Wakeham's was a drapers and outfitters called Heley and Dempsters. Later it became Thomas' and, in the 1920s, a fruit shop and greengrocers. Where the Job Centre is now used to be the Star Inn, in the middle of which was an archway where the carriages went through to the stables behind; the main entrance to this is still marked by a large stone on the pavement.

What is now Roy Doble's jewellery store was the Star Tea Company, managed by Mr Claude Colman. The building below was where Bill Rogers had his china shop. Originally this was owned by the two Hawke sisters, who kept a shoe shop and it was later converted into the Unemployment Exchange when this moved from Church Street. This, together with what was the Eddy family's pram and furnishing shop next door, is now all part of Oliver's Furniture Shop. The present-day ladies' hairdressers was Miss Curtis' Shoe Shop.

Next to this is a cobbled opening, recently named 'Cobbled Ope' by the Council, which leads to Five Wells. The well can be approached by way of a winding pathway of cobbled granite steps and there is a very interesting water trough there inscribed 'Thomas Cock, Mayor 1703'. All of the inhabitants in this area could draw water from these wells and they were very popular despite the many dung heaps which were built up by the horse owners nearby. When my brother Percy was home he

Left: *The drapers which was for many years Wakeham's chemist. The door on the left lead to a room where they ground freshly-roasted coffee beans.*

would never drink water out of the tap but preferred to go down to Five Wells to quench his thirst. When my father worked for Tonkin he had stables there, which have now been turned into a dwelling house and which it is said once belonged to the Angel Hotel across the street.

Alongside 'Cobbled Ope' is a building which has always been a private house. Mr Milne the dentist, who originally came from Scotland, lived here, and before him there was a Mr Gatro from Penzance with his surgery. Mrs Carne was caretaker of the house. Next door was Reginald Rogers, a very dignified man much interested in the history of Cornwall and Helston and who, I believe, wrote a book on Helston for the Old Cornwall Society. He was the Town Clerk and in the same building were a number of solicitors, including, in the 1930s, the Second World War hero, Lt Cdr Robert Hitchens. Hitchens had made a name for himself before the war as an international dinghy sailor and racing driver and he joined the Royal Naval Volunteer Reserve taking part in many operations in MTBs, mainly on the east and south coasts of England, before being killed by a stray bullet during an MTB (Motor Torpedo Boats) raid. The *Falmouth Packet*, reporting his death on 16 April 1943, even compared him with Sir Francis Drake and remarked: 'He lead his men into battle without weighing the odds, confident of their support in the tightest of corners'. He had won the DSO twice, the DSC three times and had been mentioned in dispatches on three occasions.

Barclays Bank lower down the street was, for quite a period of time, known as Bolitho's Bank. The Bolitho family were bankers from Penzance and originally owned the building but later sold it to Barclays. Next door to that was a private house which became the Adair Hairdressers catering for men on the ground floor and ladies on the first floor – the whole owned by a Miss Coad. In the lower part of that property were the Brown Owl Tea Rooms and next door to that a general store run by Mr Orchard, who moved there from a shop in Church Street. The building used to be Trelawney's Restaurant and before that it was a beautiful granite fronted house where the Martyn family lived. A portion of the property is now to become a pub for the town in the year 2000.

Lower down the street lived a Mr and Mrs Andrews who had a fish and chip shop and a tobacconists. Cooking was done over an oil stove in a saucepan and customers would sit and wait in the shop, which was furnished with spitoons. The next building along the street was the Regent Hotel, which later became Rosewarne's Restaurant where staff from the banks and offices of Helston took their lunch in times past. Finally it was taken over by Woolworths.

The paving slabs nearby are particularly interesting. The pattern incised on them enables the rain water to be distributed evenly and drain away more quickly, and each pavement is shaped and chiselled. Men were employed to sit down for months on end, with only an old sack beneath them for comfort, and would chisel away. Each man used his own design, hence one side of the street is quite different from the other. Some of the pavements are carved with a triangular pattern, others with circles and some with helixes. I well remember men sitting down doing such work in the 1920s when stone for the road was also broken with a long-handled sledge-hammer called a 'spall-hammer'. (If you wanted to hit something really hard we used to say 'Spall – go to 'un boy'.). Great pieces of stone were delivered by horse and cart and a man would sit there all day long, just breaking it up. Specific places were set aside for this type of work, such as a spot on top of Gweek Hill out towards Constantine, another at Mawgan and one down at Carne Creek on the road to Gillan.

E. J. ODGERS,
Plumber and General Engineer

Workshops—12 Coinagehall Street, HELSTON.
Residence—28 Coinagehall Street, HELSTON.

Hot & Cold Water Baths ; Pumps of all kinds fixed or repaired ; Acetylene Gas Lighting for Public Buildings and Private Houses ; Repairs and Work undertaken in Town or Country ; Lawn Mower Repairs and Sharpening a Speciality.
ESTIMATES SUBMITTED.

ESTABLISHED A.D. 1801
C. WAKEHAM & SON,
FAMILY & DISPENSING CHEMISTS
Coinage Hall Street, HELSTON.

Respectfully solicit your patronage and support, assuring you of their best attention to all orders entrusted to their care.
Prescriptions carefully prepared with pure Drugs and Chemicals.
Tinctures and Extracts of every kind prepared strictly according to the Pharmacopœia.
ALL THE NEW REMEDIES as introduced by the Profession.

WILLIAM J. STAPLE,
Builder, Carpenter,
Joiner & Undertaker.

JOBBING PROMPTLY ATTENDED TO.

RESIDENCE & WORKSHOPS
No. 41, COINAGE HALL STREET, HELSTON.

Helston Kennels

On either side of Coinagehall Street are Helston's attractive kennels – granite gullies carrying streams of running water. About a foot wide and nine inches deep they are placed between the pavement and the road, and are mostly edged with granite blocks. They also have cobbled bottoms. Naturally unwary motorists occasionally get their wheels trapped in these streams, but there is no doubt that they add greatly to the picturesque nature of the town and have long provided an easy means of cleaning the streets. Other towns in Cornwall have them, but nowhere is there such a network as in Helston.

I was always told that the River Cober flowed through the kennels of Helston and that before the Second World War the water was turned red by the tin washings in the Wendron area. In the Cober Valley just behind the inn at Wendron the river has been dammed to create a pool, from which leads a cleverly engineered leat that runs for at least two miles to the kennels. As it runs down the Cober Valley the leat can easily be seen at the bridge over the Cober leading to Coverack Bridges. At this point it is about three feet above the river itself and a new spillway ensures that the water flow is not excessive.

Beyond the bridge the leat leaves the Cober Valley and crosses the Redruth Road into Helston; in order for this to be possible it had to be run high up the side of Rocky Valley along the top edge of Trannack Quarry and through the farm at Trelubbas Wartha. Here it flows beside the farm entry road and then disappears into a field just where the farm road meets the old route of the Redruth Road. From there the waterway continues through a modern pipeline, although its direction follows the original route under the Lowertown Road and then along the top of a Cornish hedge.

At Water-ma-Trout, where the leat divides, is a control point where water can be switched to flow towards Helston Parish Church or towards the old Turnpike at the top of Godolphin Road. The right-hand branch towards the church can best be seen where it tumbles down beside the churchyard wall, past the Andrew Hall and down the opposite side of Church Street.

The other route is more complex; after crossing a housing estate and going underground it emerges near the top of Godolphin Road. It is an almost straight run down the left of Godolphin Road to the junction of Wendron Street and Penrose Road where it divides again. The tributary which trickles down Penrose Road then flows into Church Street to meet the water from the opposite direction. These leats combine and then flow under the street before emerging behind the

Above and left: Some of the kennels in Meneage Street.
(Main picture courtesy Gerald Trethowan)

garden of Lismore House, running under the road of Nettles Hill and back into the river.

The main kennel down Wendron Street goes into a pipe and under the road in front of the Town Hall where it divides to flow down each side of Coinagehall Street. A new kennel has recently been constructed on the eastern side of the Guildhall, enhancing that particular corner of the town.

Meneage Street also had double kennels well into the 1930s but sadly these have now gone. The original leat used to work these kennels was all part of the Wendron leat, a branch from which ran at the back of the street and parallel to Godolphin Road. From here it turned southwards and then took a right turn at the prison to run into the James' fields at the back of and parallel to Meneage Street.

It was divided once again – one section passing near the Union into Meneage Street and the other passing down at Whitehill into the start of the kennel.

Lower Coinagehall Street

Where Collins the estate agent is now, used to be a forage merchant, run by Ken Roskruge who kept his stores for animal foodstuffs at the back of the building. The little cobbled opening by the shop led back to a cottage but, due to a fire and the rebuild which followed, this has now been blocked up. Next door to Mr Roskruge there was a butchers, owned by Mr Ralph and, later, by Mr E.C. Oliver who lived at Daneville, a large house in Cross Street. The shop is now a delicatessen. Above the butchers lived a Miss Ethel Hill – the secretary for the Forester's in Helston.

Mr Wearne (who lost his leg during the First World War) lived at the top of Lady Street where he kept the only picture-framing business in town (which served Eddy & Sons, Olivers and many others). In the shop below (now an opticians and perhaps once the photographic studio of Mr Harrison) was Mr Opie the photographer. Next door to that is Chymber House, where Mr Day lived. He came from Chymber Farm at Cury and I remember him as a man with a large beard like that of his brother who lived at Park Sledge.

Just past Chymber House there is a recess and a house with steps leading up to the front door protected by railings. I believe that this used to be Miss Barker's Finishing School for young ladies, run on the site of the original grammar school. Here also was a little ironmongery where one could buy paraffin and general hardware from a lady called Williams who may well have had connections with the foundry at the back. The foundry owner's son, Johnny Williams, went to work as a plumber for the Gas Board when the business closed and was always known as Johnny Geek because of the way he laughed. Miss Wakeham, whose home, Leslie House, faced Johnnie's own little upstairs flat, once sent for him to complain of an awful smell of gas in the air. 'I'll soon settle that', Johnny assured her, upon which he lit a match and was blown, with Miss Wakeham, out through the French windows onto the lawn! The road leading up to the foundry was known as Foundry Hill; today this takes one instead to a little housing estate known as Champions Yard.

Living in the end house on the corner of Coinagehall Street and Nettle's Hill was a Miss Best. When the council opted to build the toilets opposite, she vowed to draw her blinds and never open them again, and she did just that, keeping her promise until the day she died. To the right of the monument next to the Bowling Green is a fine house where Colonel Head the veterinary surgeon lived. He married a Miss Hoadley, who was the daughter of a Helston vet. The couple had two sons, Charles and Jack, and their grandson John now runs the business.

At the bottom of Coinagehall Street is the magnificent Grylls Monument; a granite ashlar arch, strongly buttressed and finished with four octagonal pinnacles. The original protective railings were removed during the Second World War to be used as scrap iron but they have now been replaced. Some 196 tons of the finest granite were used to build the monument and the cost was met by 2386 people all keen to pay homage to the man who had been instrumental in keeping open the threatened Wheal Vore tin mine. The inscription reads: 'To the memory of Humphrey Millet Grylls. Raised by Subscription MDCCCXXXIV.'

The nearby bowling green directly behind the monument is reputed to be the oldest in Cornwall, dating from 1760. It was formerly the site of the royal castle, the residence of Reginald, Earl of Cornwall. This was in ruins prior to the time of Edward IV, and no trace can now be seen. From one corner of the bowling green one can get a good view of St Johns and the land below.

Looking up Coinagehall Street there are four houses on the right hand side, the first of which is now Mitchell's Estate Agent. This used to be the Penrose Estate Office and was at one time occupied by one or two of the Trengrouse sisters. A little higher up the street is the 15th-century Blue Anchor pub (*below*) – Helston's oldest inn and renowned worldwide for its home brew. Known locally as springo, the drink has become a firm favourite with locals and visitors alike. The inn is also well known for its old skittle alley which dates back to very early times. It has recently been refurbished and much of its old character retained. The Anchor has for many years been kept by the Richards family but during my childhood I remember a short little man there – a real character who always referred to himself as Sergeant Menadue and strutted along with a military gait. He claimed that he was the brewer for the pub, but of course he only gave Mr Richards a hand.

Just before the chapel on the right of the street is a row of cottages leading to the Epworth Hall (the original chapel). At the end of the street there was a sweet shop kept by a Mrs Rowe whose daughter married Jack Rogers – the man who turned the little cottage next door into a betting office.

Upper Coinagehall Street, 1939.
The man with the barrow is Mr Edgecumbe who sold cockles and muscles.

Farmers driving their sheep to market, c.1930s.

T & T Garage, Coinagehall Street, here promoting Ford cars. The man behind the letter 'C' is Mr Reggie Simpson, the joint owner of the garage. The building was demolished in the late 1950s in order to provide space for the building of the new General Post Office.

Late 19th-century photograph of a donkey and trap (or 'jingle') in Coinagehall Street.

Bowling club members with the Grylls Monument behind, c.1905.

Lawn tennis on the bowling green, mid 1920s.

Grylls Monument, 1910.

The Blue Anchor Skittle Club. Left to right, standing: Ned Richardson, ? Angove, Bill Lethbridge, ? Williams, Jim Smith, G. Paynter, William Harris, ?, Tom Richardson, Fred Philpot, ?, Reg James; front: Henry Prisk, Bill James, Charlie Paynter, John Winn (with ball), Sam Real.

One shop up from the chapel was that of Mr White of White Hill – originally built for Mr James the pork butcher. Next door to that is the old Alpha Hotel, kept by Alfred Pascoe. It was here (or otherwise at the Regent) that most of the sales representatives stayed whilst visiting the town's shops. In those days they came in mostly by train and then caught the bus to Falmouth, Penzance or elsewhere. Holiday makers seldom stayed at the Alpha, most heading instead for the Poldhu and other hotels at the coast. The opening next door to the Alpha Hotel led to stabling on the right of which was a little doorway to Dr Elliston's surgery. Dr Elliston was a very brusque man, but kind; whenever he came to see one of us my mother would take out her purse to pay him and he would say 'No Laura, somebody else can pay that for you.' He never took a penny, maintaining the belief that those who had the money should pay for it. Father suffered from malaria and ague and would lie in bed shivering and shaking all over. The disease left him with a tendency to terrible headaches, from which he sought relief by a visit to Dr Elliston. 'I can't do anything for you, Jenkin,' came the doctor's reply, 'the only remedy I can suggest is keep your bowels open and trust in the Lord!' That was the end of Father's relationship with the good doctor. He came home as mad as fire, vowed never to go to him again and changed to Dr Michael's list although the rest of the family always saw Dr Elliston.

The Fitzsimmons Arms (formerly the Seven Stars Inn) is immediately next door and I remember an Irish family called Murphy running this establishment. A Catholic couple, Mr and Mrs Murphy used to get the father from the Catholic church at Mullion to come in and take mass in the inn, a practice which may have been the catalyst for the rebirth of the Catholic Church in Helston.

The next block of buildings contains the Pizza Shop (once Anthony's Fruit Shop) and the Coffee Bean. The latter was Mr Wills' restaurant which, despite being a little primitive, was where many of the farmers went at Monday lunchtime when he cooked roast beef. Mr Wills would stand at the epps door (stable door) wearing his white apron, waiting for his customers to come. They would sit on forms at one long, central table whilst their host carved slices of fine-looking beef. The smell wafting from the open doorway was ''ansom'.

This opening led to the old West Briton office. Note the metal rails on either side of the path, protecting the edges of the flagstones against undue wear by the horses and carts.

The three-storey building next door houses the Post Office where, in the early 1900s, the Heynes family had one of the many grocery stores which they ran throughout Cornwall. After the First World War Mr Jackett Simpson acquired the site and converted it to a garage with petrol pumps out on the pavement. All of the repair work was done at the back of the building, under the name of T & T Motor Works and the Post Office now keeps its vans garaged in the old workshop area. Higher up the street is an arcade of shops which at one time was the Prince's Arms, owned by Redruth Brewery. It was empty for a while in the early 1920s before Mr Pill, the brewery's agent, asked my father to go and re-open it. As a child of six or seven I can remember going there with my brothers and running through the empty building. After the war, it was closed as a pub and the firm of Russell Knights took over the premises, removing the granite front windows and door before putting in a new shop front for a drapery. When they left it was converted to an arcade of shops.

Just before the Angel is the site where Tommy Willy kept his newspaper shop and wool store. Before that Griffiths & Leaver had a cycle shop and stores there. The Angel Hotel has changed very little externally and was once the town house of the celebrated Godolphin family. It still retains its Tudor doorway and centuries-old features, including an indoor well and, at the rear of the building, is a Georgian assembly room with a minstrels' gallery. The Godolphins' country home, which dates from Elizabethan times, was in the village of Godolphin about four miles west of Helston and was owned by the family from the 16th century until the death of Francis, Earl of Godolphin, in 1766. The Godolphins worshipped at nearby Breage Church, and it was there that Margaret Godolphin, wife of Sidney, Lord High Treasurer of England, was buried in 1678.

After Helston returned two members to Parliament in 1298 and until 1832, voters were often taken to the Angel and entertained to induce them to vote for the nominee of the Godolphins, who paid the rates for the whole of the borough in return for the right to nominate two MPs. When the family gave up the premises it became known as the Angel Inn and Tavern. It featured prominently in the social, municipal and political

history of the borough and in early Victorian days was also used for the Ecclesiastical Courts.

Above the Angel was the drapery belonging to the Oxenhams (and before that to Mr Dale). It was a thriving business and there was quite a large staff there. An opening by the shop now leads to the lower car park but at one time it led to the plumbers run by Ernie Hodges and Johnny Williams. My elder sister worked for some time for Mr Eddy in the shop next door (who, in addition to his paint and wallpaper, also sold children's toys). In 1936 he relocated to Meneage Street, where his grandsons now carry on the business.

Simpson's outfitters occupied the next shop from 1912 until 1998 and always supplied the top hats and tails for Flora Day. The shop was originally run by Mr Winkworth, and when the family lived above the shop, Tommy Holland (*see page 19*) lived there with them. I was shown a letter written by Mrs Winkworth to the Holland family in Canada explaining that her husband had died and that she would be moving back to her native Penzance to live. The Winkworths moved out and the Simpsons, who were also a Penzance family, moved in.

Another opening (*opposite*) lead to the old *West Briton* office, which is now located at the top of Meneage Street near Trengrouse Way. An interesting feature of this opening are the metal rails at floor level, on either side of the path, meant to protect the edges of the flagstones against excessive wear by the horses and carts. Higher up the opening, again in the floor, there are two mill stones (*above*) but whether or not there was a mill being run there at some stage has not been discovered.

The shop next door (now selling cards) was, at one time, a retail shop for Trounson's the grocers. They were in business in a big way, acting as wholesalers and retailers, supplying all of the other grocery shops in the town. The wholesale business and a bakehouse were further down Coinagehall Street at the back of what was the Prince's Arms (now the Arcade). The Trounsons had all their offices in Church Street. A Redruth firm, they took over the business from a man called Martin and kept their lorries in the yard to the rear of the offices. The three drivers were Stanley Ashton, another man called Martin from Lowertown, and Bill Coles. In the Coinagehall Street shop there was a staff of ten, and at Church Street in the offices there was another staff of about ten under the charge of Mr Alfred Oates. My father worked at Trounson's Wholesale Department for several years as a storeman. The yard was a hive of activity and Mr Edgar Trounson used to come around on Saturdays, when it was particularly busy, to make sure that everybody was satisfied with what they had purchased. Personal service was very much to the fore. My cousin, Gwen James, always remembered the small poke of sweets enclosed with the order every week which was always delivered to 17 Godolphin Road by a boy riding a bicycle fitted with a basket on the front.

The present O'Donavan's used to be Carne's Tap, run by a Falmouth family firm who at one time kept the Bell Hotel. One of their relatives was Major Carne of the Glorious Gloucesters who received the Victoria Cross in Korea. Next up the street is E.T.S. (Electrical Technical Service) which, around 1900, was the boot and shoe shop of S. Row & Co. A Mr Upex came to Helston as an officer in the Salvation Army and took over the shop, later turning it into one of the first radio and electrical outlets in town. He also used the shop as a depot for the old Cornwall Motor Transport buses. If one wanted to send a parcel out to Manaccan, one took it into the shop, paid the delivery charge of threepence, and the bus would come down from the station to pick it up.

Immediately next door is the Midland Bank, now named HRSC. In the late 1800s this was Cunnacks Printers and the 1891 census shows a Miss Cunnack still living above the shop. In the 1920s it was Miss Barker's newsagency and then the bank took it over. Ward Cornwall used the first floor as their offices, and on the site of the cash-dispensing till there was an opening leading up to the rooms. At this point one arrives once again at Boots Corner (now Yates Estate Agent).

Wesleyan Chapel

Methodism first came to Helston in 1755 when John Wesley visited the town. The Coinagehall Street Wesleyan Chapel is a very fine example of 19th-century architecture. It is built of granite and Plymouth limestone and is a distinct asset to the town. Erected in 1888 by Mr W. J. Winn, at a cost of £5000, it was designed to seat around 1000 people. The pulpit was made by Reggie's uncle, Ernie James, and the trustees of the time, in appreciation of the work he did, gave him a silver watch suitably inscribed. In the early 1990s the interior was completely renovated with much of the cost being raised by public subscription. The chapel includes a fine entrance hall and a grand stairway (as well as a lift) leading to a delightful chapel on the first floor, with a beautiful ceiling and the original organ; the ground floor has a kitchen and a suite of committee rooms.

Above: *Children at the Coingagehall Street Wesleyan Chapel, 1908. The picture includes Reggie Jenkin's cousin, Gwendolin James.*

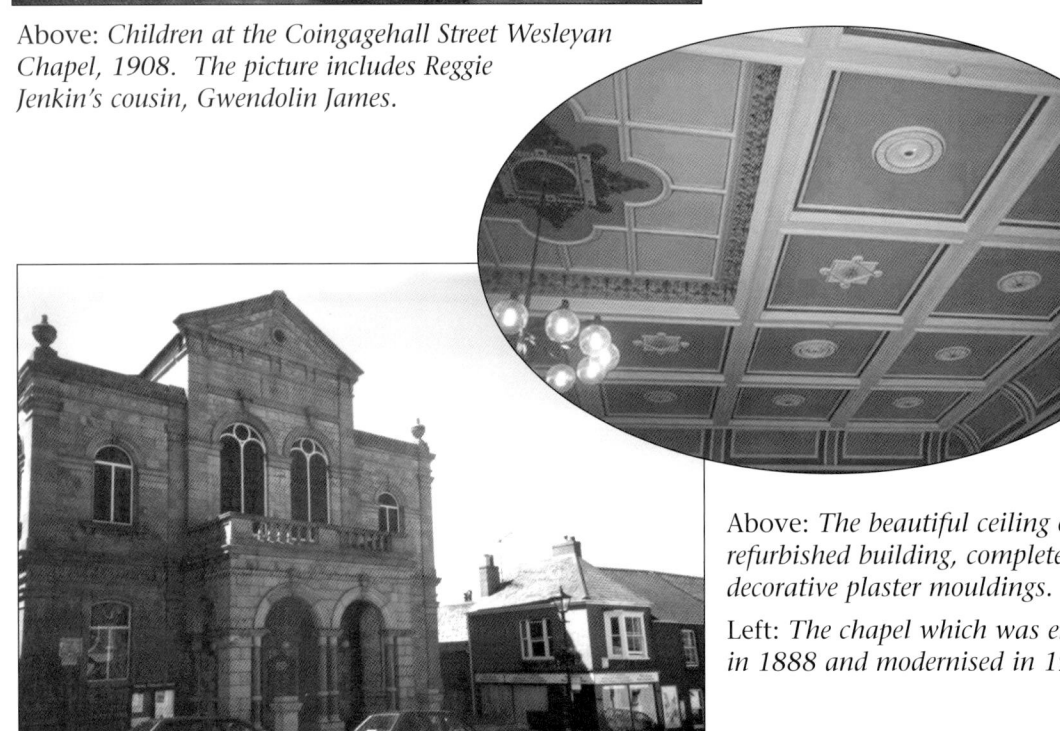

Above: *The beautiful ceiling of the refurbished building, complete with decorative plaster mouldings.*

Left: *The chapel which was erected in 1888 and modernised in 1993.*

Helpers at the Helston Wesley Canteen, 1942. Left to right, back: Mrs Gibson, Miss A. Hendy, Mrs Crute, Miss Martin, Mrs Hart, Mrs Williams, Mrs Johns, Mrs Chanter, Mrs Lyne; front: Mrs Jeffery, Miss Lewis, Miss Kneebone, Mrs Reed, Mrs Marton, Miss Richards, Mrs Pollard, Mrs Jennings, Mrs Watermouth.

Children's Opening Day at the chapel in 1905.
Gwendoline James (Reg's cousin) is far left, second row from the front with the bow in her hair. Lily and Erna Jenkin (Reg's half sisters) are in the centre of the fourth row from the front with their sashes clearly visible. Reg's other half sister, Mary Jenkin, is standing to the right of the lady holding the baby to the front of the group.

Members of Helston Wesley Chapel photographed mid 1920s at Danville, Cross Street, the home of Mr and Mrs E.C. Oliver. Left to right, back (standing): ?, ?, Mrs Kneebone, ?, ?, Mrs Alfred Oates, ?, ?, ?, ?, Miss Gwen James, Mr Dawson's son, ?, ?; third row (seated): Mr Fred Thomas, ?, ?, ?, Mrs Fred James, Mr Fred James; second row (seated): Mr Fred Thomas, E.C. Oliver, Miss Julian, Miss Downing, ?, ?, ?, ?, Mrs Taskis; front: ?, ?, ?, Miss Lewis, Mr Dawson, ?, ?, ?.

Looking towards the church up Church Street, early 1900s. Lander's shop is on the right hand side with the bay window.

Church Street

Church Street is a quaint old street which retains many of its original features. Wakeham's Chemist on the corner was the original Stamp Office and faced the Guildhall under which was the fire station. The fire bell was at the top end of the Market House and the horses for drawing the engine were either kept up in the Angel Stables and in a field behind the church. It was a very steep hill leading out of the station and the horses must have been under some strain. When the brigade began to use a motorised engine, they had to get up steam to work the water pumps.

The Red Lion in Church Street was kept by a good-natured couple called Mr and Mrs Sweeney. Next door to them was the shop of John Kemp Bray who started up in Meneage Road with a smallholding and a shop selling boots and shoes, later moving to Church Street. He used to travel around the markets selling his 'Holdfast Boots' and shoes from a motorised van. Later his shop became a furnishing store. Immediately adjacent is Wheelbarrow Lane, a winding cobbled path with shallow steps leading to Five Wells. The lane was so called because each step was shaped to allow easier passage for the wheels of the barrows which were pushed up and down the hill. The next house was home to the Hoadleys, one of whom married Colonel Head, the vet.

At the back of the electrical shop is Five Well Lane – a strange name as there appears to be only one well here. Old maps reveal that there was, at one time, a dispensary there, where people who could not afford to pay a doctor received free medicines. Could this have been at No. 5? If so, it could be that with so many references to visiting '5 Well Lane' the thoroughfare itself eventually took on the name.

Above: *Wheelbarrow Lane.*
Below: *Church Street showing the Trustees Bank on the right and Pengelly's shop on the left, 1920s.*

The big granite building on the left (which has been converted into flats) was a National Children's Home. When this closed in the early 1920s, all the children were transferred to the Union, where they became part of the Workhouse. The British Legion then used the vacated building as a club, of which, in 1925, my father was caretaker.

At the other end of the street, up Church Hill, is the Old National School, now 'Andrew Hall', one of a fine group of Georgian buildings. Mr Andrew was church organist and his wife was very much involved in all church activities. They lived on Falmouth Road and when the school came up for sale, Mr Andrew lent the money, interest free, for the church's purchase of the building.

Church Street Chapel drama production, 1926.
Left to right, standing: Effie Rogers, Ida Carlyon, Ethel Bray, Olive ?, Miss Burrows, Audrey Old;
seated: Michael Bray, Erna Jenkin, Miss Adams.

Another production in the same year.
Left to right, back: Kit Rows, Miss Edith Winn, Miss Burrows, Frank Cunnack;
middle: Miss ? Adams, Effie Rogers, Minnie Carlyon, Ethel Bray, Ida Carlyon, May Rogers;
front: ?, ? Pearce.

St Michael's Church, 1900. Note the farm in the background which has now been replaced by houses.

Centre of Helston, c.1900, taken from the tower of St Michael's. The Passmore Edwards Science and Arts building is the twin-gabled feature left of the centre background, to its right is the Market House (which is now the Museum). The Willows is in the centre foreground.

St Michael's Church

Above right: *Interior of the old St Michael's Church, Helston.*

Above: *Andrew Hall.*

Above: *Helston Church Bellringers, 1951. The photograph includes Clifford Willy, Clifford Liddicoat, Jack Read, Harry Williams, Tom Pascoe, Terrance Williams, WREN (RNAS Culdrose), Jack Curtis, Roger Stephens, Dennis Endean, Walter Liddicoat, Dick Pascoe and Lionel Endean.*

Left: *Helston Church Bible Class, 1937. Left to right, back: Jack Crowle, Stan Miles, Clifford Liddicoat, Stan Thomas, Frank Wearne; 5th row: B. Rowe, Lionel Johns, Jim Bassett; 4th row: Ken Johns, Hubert Pearce, Walter Williams; 3rd row: R. Thomas, P. Williams, D. Courtis, D. Haynes; 2nd row: B. Tucker, N. Williams, I. Woods, S. Martin, J. Tonkin; front: K. Pasco, T. Williams, L. Bowden, R. Bassett.*

Below: *A well-maintained iron headstone in the churchyard. The skull and crossbones is the old sign of a blacksmith.*

In 1910 the school was a public elementary school. It was erected and endowed in 1828 for 300 children with Miss Trevenning of Cross Street as the headteacher. A new boys' school was built in 1894 for 183 pupils on a site given by Captain Rogers JP and in 1910 Mr Bernard Rawlings was the master. Both schools were vacated in 1956 in favour of new buildings on the other side of town. The Old National School served several generations of Helston children, including many 21st-century residents of the town. In 1956, the freehold was acquired by Russell Knights, House Furnishers of Coinagehall Street, and used as storage space for shop goods. In 1984 it was taken on by Harvey Pentreath, Rector of St Michael's, Helston, on behalf of the Parochial Church Council. The intention was to completely restore the old school building and bring it back to its original condition, re-designing and equipping the interior to serve the needs of both the church and the community as a whole.

The restoration included a total refurbishment inside and out. The roof was entirely stripped off and reconstructed and the walls were picked out and repointed. Gutters and downpipes were renewed and the woodwork overhauled. On the ground floor, a fine reception hall was constructed, supported by kitchen and toilet facilities. A wide staircase was built to give internal access to the upper floor, which comprised three separate areas (these being the original classrooms). The stairs open into a reception area with refreshment facilities and an office. The two remaining classrooms were remodelled to meet the requirements of meetings, group activities, Sunday schools and other users. Both floors can be used independently. The ground floor is approached through the doors in the courtyard, whilst the upper floor is approached by means of covered steps in the cottage yard and by means of a pedestrian bridge spanning the gap separating the main building from the churchyard. This sensitive renovation has preserved a unique Georgian complex with modern facilities for the town.

Adjacent to the hall is St Michael's Church which is constructed of stone from Tregonning Hill, just west of Helston near Godolphin House. The tower, 103 feet in height, is of granite ashlar and is finished with a parapet of quatrefoil work and pinnacles on a corbel table. The tower contains a very fine peal of eight bells. Almost opposite the main door of the church can be seen the tomb of Henry Trengrouse. The present church was built in the 18th century to replace the 12th-century building which was struck by lightning in 1727. The cost of the rebuilding was met by Francis, Earl of Godolphin, who also gave as a gift an imposing brass chandelier dated 1763. The beautiful east window was donated in the 1930s

Top: *The Willows*.
Above: *United Methodist Church, 'The Little Ship', 1958. The building was demolished in the mid 1960s. Today the remains of the walls can still be seen supporting a private car park.*

to replace the original window depicting the Transfiguration, which had been damaged by a storm. The new piece shows the risen and ascended Lord in glory, surrounded by angels dancing the Furry Dance, with the notes of the dance curled around them. In the middle of the window is a picture of Mary holding the infant Jesus and at the bottom is a picture of St Michael slaying the dragon, with St Michael's Mount as a background. The original East window has been re-erected on the south side of the church.

In June 1970 a structural fault was discovered in the chancel arch and the architect and structural engineers condemned the building as unsafe, ordering it to be closed within a fortnight. Both the Methodist and Catholic institutions of Helston were swift to ask what they could do to help and the church requested, and were immediately granted, the use of St Mary's Church for its parish communion and the chance to join with the Methodist evening worship. These happy arrangements continued for the next two years and spoke volumes for the congregations of all three churches with never a word of

Above: *Modern-day Lower Church Street. The van on the left is at the entrance to St James Place.*

Above right: *Wheelbarrow Lane.*

Right: *Market House – now the Museum. The entrance to the old market building was constructed in 1837–38. One room of the building on the left housed the Trustee Savings Bank. The gun was lifted from the wreck of the Anson which went ashore on Loe Bar.*

criticism during that period. The church re-opened with a special service on 18 June 1972 lead by the Rt Revd Maurice Key, Bishop of Truro. The installation of girders allowed the arch to be kept open and the interior was carefully adapted to create a building which had roots in the past and in the hearts of Helston people, but which was more suitable for the needs of the 20th century.

Designed by William Wood, an architect and builder from Truro, The Willows, erected in 1776, is a fine example of a Georgian town house. Wood began his career as an apprentice to John Bland, who built Helston Church under the supervision of Thomas Edwards of Greenwich. The Willows was built as No. 35 Church Street for Thomas Glynn, five times Mayor of Helston. In the original design the front wall was to be faced in Breage granite, but in the final building this was changed to Newham stone. There were plans for 'two parlours and library with dado and neat wooden mouldings with mahogany sashes and with best framed windows'. By 1806 Thomas' nephew, R.G. Grylls, was living there and he completely refurbished the interior of the house. In later years it became the residence of Sir Henry Toy the banker. In 1934 Helston Rural District Council gave way to Kerrier Rural District Council (which was the same as the old RDC less Porthleven and included parts of Falmouth and Redruth rural districts). The newly-formed council bought The Willows from the representatives of the late Sir Henry Toy for their new council offices (*see page 89*). Little of the original interior detail survives, but the exterior, with two ground-floor canted bays either side of a central pedimented doorcase, still presents an impressive front to the street. From the upper windows Council Members and friends gather on 8 May for a wonderful view of the Flora Day dancers coming down Church Street and entering the gardens of Lismore.

The memorial to Henry Trengrouse, who perfected both the Breeches Buoy and the Live Spencer life-saving apparatus.

CROSS STREET

Church Lane

Cross Street, so named after the Celtic cross outside No. 1, includes in its length some of Helston's finest houses. It has seen little change over the last century and remains a delightful area of the town, its old-fashioned lamps making for an enchanting evening stroll.

Three of its best houses date from the 18th century and were built for a group of closely related lawyers and bankers with business interests in mining. No. 5, known as the Great Office, was the premises of a firm of solicitors, the partners of which were all related to one another from 1756 to 1934 (and who administered the Duke of Leeds' (Godolphin) estates). No. 5 was also the headquarters of the Union Bank, founded in 1788 by Thomas Glynn (1744–94) and his nephew Thomas Grylls (1760–1813).

No. 1 Cross Street, dating from the 18th century, commands a fine view along the street. The ceiling of its parlour is decorated with handsome plasterwork depicting shells and dolphins, and the overmantle painting of a Naval scene is dated c.1780 – probably an accurate dating for the house itself. Its porch, however, was added in the early 19th century. No. 3, a tall, three-storeyed house with a fine bracketed cornice, belonged to the Glynn family.

No. 4 Cross Street is one of the most elegant houses in Helston and has a remarkable resemblance to Bonython, the country home of John Trevenen (1751–1825), a partner in the Union Bank and a cousin to Mrs Borlase. It is a south-facing, two-storey construction of local Breage granite (silvery-grey in colour) and has five pairs of windows – the central pair projecting slightly under a triangular pediment. A Venetian window, similar to the two in No. 35 Church Street, lights the large open-well staircase. In 1838 John Borlase occupied the house – shortly, it is thought, after his marriage to Elizabeth Bolitho, and just five years before his death in 1845. John too was a partner in the firm of solicitors at Great Office.

In 1817 George Simon Borlase, son of John, married Thomas Grylls' daughter Emily. At about the same time he substantially rebuilt No. 11 opposite No. 4, adding a delightful rusticated doorcase to the street. His brother-in-law, Glynn Grylls, who died in 1866, also busied himself with additions to the street, building, in 1838, a 'small' villa which became No. 2 and where he laid out a fashionable garden of four acres directly opposite the Great Office. A fine example of early Victorian architecture, No. 2 is now known as Lismore and its beautiful railings decorated with pine cones are an excellent example of art nouveau. Later, it became the home of the late Doctor Michael who for many years was a much-loved and respected doctor in the town. His widow used to lead the dancers around the garden on Flora Day (when the house is open to visitors), thus starting a tradition which still continues today – the dancers taking refreshments and a short, well-earned rest in the beautiful settings of the house. A meandering path leads around a sloping lawn bordered by a large pond, and enters, through a rockwork archway, a shady dell where there is a delightful bark summerhouse. The proximity of the town is easily forgotten here where the atmosphere is one of comfortable, substantial privacy. An extensive flower garden was built between No. 2 and No. 4 and the southern section made into a kitchen garden, with a stable block beyond.

Church Lane, which leads from the back of St Michael's Church and down into Cross Street is the only bridleway in the town and is often noted for the beautiful cobweb patterns on its granite paving stones. Almost opposite Church Lane is Tanyard Lane, named after the old tannery which is now incorporated in the Royal British Legion Club. Cunnacks had a slaughterhouse down on Helston Moors (an area popular with walkers) and the hides were brought up to the tannery for treating, some then being taken to the Meneage Street drying rooms.

No. 10 Cross Street bears the date 1783 on its granite walls, and is a modestly-scaled, two-storey building. Later in the same century, a three-storey wing was added to the southern, sloping side of the house. The garden elevation has two Venetian windows, one above the other.

Penhellis (which is built on the site of a former farm) is an Italianate villa on the high ground at Cross Street's eastern end where undeveloped paddocks and fields remain between the site and the church behind the Great Office. The villa was designed in 1840 by the architect Wightwick for a Frederick Hill (who died in 1874), the brother-in-law of Glynn Grylls. Hill became a partner of the solicitors' firm at Great Office and the practice became known as Grylls & Hill. Six years before building Penhellis, Wrightwick had also served as the architect for the monumental arch in Coinagehall Street, erected in memory of another member of the Grylls family, Humphrey Millet Grylls, the eldest son of Thomas Grylls. Mill Lane, at the foot of Penhellis Hill, passes what was the old town mill and leads to Helston Moors.

CROSS STREET

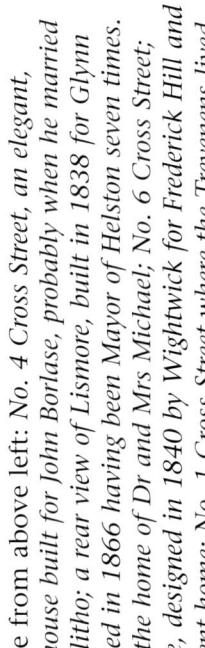

Clockwise from above left: *No. 4 Cross Street, an elegant, south-facing house built for John Borlase, probably when he married Elizabeth Bolitho; a rear view of Lismore, built in 1838 for Glynn Grylls, who died in 1866 having been Mayor of Helston seven times. It was later the home of Dr and Mrs Michael; No. 6 Cross Street; Penhellis House, designed in 1840 by Wightwick for Frederick Hill and now a retirement home; No. 1 Cross Street where the Trevenens lived, followed by Dr Brooke and Dr Willis; Great Office where the Duke of Leeds' estate was admininstered;*

St John's

Directly behind the Grylls Monument, at the western end of Coinagehall Street, is the ancient bowling green from which one can enjoy a fine view of St Johns, the oldest part of town where there was once an old Priory and leper hospital. When the hospital was dissolved in 1545, only the chapel continued to function, serving as a convenient place of rest for the weary or sick traveller journeying to or from St Michael's Mount at Marazion.

Around the corner from the monument Mr Billing built a bungalow where he sold ice-cream. He was also a keen radio enthusiast and re-charged accumulators for other people's radio sets. The site on the left on the corner of Bullock Lane was a smithy kept by a Mr Bennetts. Mr Chanter lived in the house opposite and the yard which has now been developed was Harvey's Coal Yard. When the Harveys moved out it became a garage, then an agricultural machinery business and, subsequently, the premises of South West Power Tools. The houses which now stand on the site are known collectively as Medlyn Court.

During my youth, Furry Way was still just a collection of open fields. Turning the corner to take the Porthleven road there were five cottages called Mason's Row, with their toilets backing out on to the footpath. Part of the Penrose Estate, the cottages housed masons and other workmen. Coronation Lake and Park (which opened on 20 July 1912 in commemoration of the coronation of King George V) was formerly a piece of common ground where the townspeople grazed their ponies and donkeys. The lake is now provided with hire boats and is a haven for many wild birds, in particular ducks, which breed here in great numbers, and swans – always a great attraction with the public. There is also a children's play area. The lake was the brainchild of Mr W.J. Winn, Borough Surveyor for the town. His son, Ernest Winn, continued the business and had a huge workshop and staff at St Johns where Uncle Ernie was the foreman.

The market was divided into two with the cattle market itself on the right hand side of the road (as one looks towards Penzance) and the area for the buying and selling of calves, pigs and chickens on the left (where the entire Monday market is now run). At the beginning of the 21st century the market's future seems uncertain and the farmers do not believe that it will survive for much longer. Should it close, a traditional part of Helston life will have come to an end after nearly seven centuries. In a charter of 1336, the town was granted four annual fairs, of which only two now survive. One such is the Harvest Fair, held on the first Monday in September (although, according to the charter, this should be the Monday nearest to 9 September). Known locally as Plum Fair because of the vast number of plums which are sold during the day, the event sees the streets lined with stalls stocked with all kinds of wares. From time immemorial there has also been a brisk trade in horses and ponies in Helston; horse dealers came from all over Cornwall to sell their animals in the town, but in recent years trading has declined significantly.

Just past the cattle market on the right was the old gasometer alongside the old Arlington Garage, originally owned by Mr Leonard Christophers. This gentleman had a number of lorries which were taken all over West Cornwall collecting milk in ten-gallon churns from the farms and delivering them to the factory for milk processing. The gasometer was erected in the early 1920s (although Helston was lit by gas from the early 1800s) and the gas works stopped working in the 1960s. The smell down there was awful. I remember my father painting the roof of our garden workshop with tar. We also used to go down there to buy coke (cheaper and cleaner than coal) which we brought home in a hand-sack trolley and burnt with the coal in the Cornish range.

Beyond the gasometer at the bridge on the main Penzance road there was only the Toll House. Beyond the Toll House is Sithney Common Hill, on the side of which is the old road that used to go up to Porthleven by way of St

Left: *The Freemasons Hall, once the Commercial School built on land given by the Duke of Leeds, and, for a time, the Wesleyan Day School.*

Right: *The Blackmore family at St Johns Bridge Toll House. Included are the five sisters Rene, Annie, Lilly, Edith and Evelyn. Lilly is the mother of the three Beare sisters whose father drove the railway station horse bus.*

Lower Green where the Coronation Lake was built in 1912.

Cottages at the bottom of Sithney Common Hill showing the James' shop, 1912, in the centre of the picture. Smith's blacksmith's buildings can be seen furthest up the road from the camera. The premises were bought by Mr R.H. Reed and a bungalow was built on the site.

St Johns Bridge over the River Cober.

Helston's first Wesleyan chapel at St Johns. The white house in the background is where the Blackmore family had their shop.

Official opening of the Coronation Lake, 1912.

The Coronation Lake.

Above left: *Helston's Handwriting School at the bottom of Lady Street opposite Leslie House where William Clifton Odger taught 50 pupils (mostly boys). He gave lessons in writing, arithmetic, grammar, geography and English history and his pupils were acknowledged as the best penmen about.*
Above right: *An old cottage looking up Old Hill.*

Elvan. One can walk up there although it is not drivable. The mill on the left of the new road was where bark tannin was produced for the tannery.

On the left over the bridge was the working men's club, run in the old chapel, converted by Johnny Adams. Mayor of Helston, Johnny lived in the farm further down the road and, as well as converting the club, he also raised money for the games equipment in Coronation Park (where a memorial to him now stands). Opposite the club there were once two little cottages.

Above the quarry in St Johns stands the Freemasons Hall – once the site of the 'Commercial School'. In 1826 a group of men of good standing in the town met together to seek subscriptions to start the establishment. They raised £700 and, after receiving additional help from the Duke of Leeds, secured a suitable site for the building. The land having been given, the school was erected and in 1827 the seven trustees appointed Mr J.G. Barnes of Birmingham as headmaster. The new style of education had a strong appeal amongst most of the middle-class parents of Helston and by 1833 the school had 60 boys on its list, some 20 of whom were boarders. Unfortunately, however, Mr Barnes made what was seen as a grave political error in the 1837 general election by voting against the Conservative candidate. The trustees of the school dismissed him from the post of headmaster and in due course it became the Wesleyan Methodist Day School before it transferred to the Union Building in Wendron Street. Finally the building became the Freemasons Hall.

The steps leading down from the hall are known as 'Drippy Droppy Steps', because of the water that continually runs over them. At the bottom of these steps and along to the left one arrives at Almshouse Hill where my Uncle Ernie was born. From Almshouse Hill, where little has altered, one passes into Nettle's Hill on the right and Foundry Hill on the left. Nettle Hill leads to the Monument at the bottom of Coinagehall Street. Foundry Hill takes its name from Williams' Foundry which occupied the site of the present Champion's Court. Throughout the Lizard one still sees evidence of Williams' work, particularly on the many pumps and signposts which would have been forged here.

After the departure of Mr Williams, the foundry was used as a smithy kept by a man called Champion' from Breage or Ashton. An old workhouse once stood near the foundry, as also did St Mary's Convent. In 1761 there was an old bell foundry in this area (although exactly where is not known) and three of its bells are still in use, two at Cury and one at Stithians. Further up the road one comes to the other end of Tanyard Lane. Up on the right is what we used to call Washer Women's Row, where the women did the laundry for Helston's hotels and richer households.

Top: *Vegetables were once washed in the Cober ready for market.*
Above: *Washer Women's Row.*

For King and Country

The Fallen from the First World War, listed on Helston War Memorial

Face One	Face Two	Face Three	Face Four
Adams, Lewis	Courtier, Foster	Moon, Phillip H.	Symons, Samuel J.
Addison, Eddie	Cunnack, George J.	Newman, Charles H.	Treloar, William
Angrove, F.C.	Granvilles, S. Raymond N.	Osmand, Thomas	Trethowan, Vyvyan
Anthony, W. Henry	Hall, Sam	Pascoe, Edward	Tyacke, C. Noel W.
Barber, Arthur	Harris, Frederick C.	Pascoe, Edwin J.	Vawse, Thomas
Barber, Leonard	Harris, W.H.	Pascoe Harry	Virgin, Percy
Bassett, T. John	Hawke, Jack	Pascoe, Herbert	Visick, Williams
Beare, Henry	Heath, Francis	Paul, William H.	White, George
Beare, W, Reginald	Heath, William A.	Perry, W. Vivian	Williams, James
Bickle, Thomas, J.	James, Richard J.	Polglase, Harry	Williams, James H.
Bray, William, K.	Jewell, James	Richards, Leslie	Williams, John W.
Cara, T. Alfred	Lukies, William J.	Silvester, William E.	Williams, William J.
Channon, Henry	Manning, T.	Smith, E.H.	Winn, Arthur
Chenoweth, Thomas J.	Matthews, Cecil	Smith, H.	Adams, Willie H.
Coupland-Smith, Vivian	Moon, Frederick J.	Stephens, Leslie	

Above left: *Those who returned to the town from the First World War together with the welcoming group at Church Street Chapel. This photograph includes the Eva twins, sons of Philemon Eva who farmed Tregarrick. One son, Richard, remained on the farm to help his father and the other twin, Thomas, was called to the Colours. He became Sergeant Farrier and was much involved in shoeing horses, many of which had been shipped over from Canada.*

Helston men who lost their lives in the 1939-45 war

Roy Anthony, Fred Anthony, William Laity, John Opie, William Penlerick, Eric Polkinhorne, James Reynolds, Douglas Stephens, John Stephens, Ronald Sturgess, Benjamin Thomas, Walter Tossell, Roy Tuppen, Montague Barrett, Ronald Kempthorne, Fredrick Hocking, Walter Williams and Douglas Collins.

For Queen and Country

On March 22 2003 at 4.25 am, two days after the invasion of Iraq, two naval helicopters crashed in the Gulf.
The seven aircrew from 849 squadron based at the Royal Naval Air Station Culdrose, who died were: *Lieutenant Philip Green, 31, of Caythorpe, Lincolnshire; Lieutenant Tony King, 35, of Helston, Cornwall; Lieutenant James Williams, 28, of Falmouth, Cornwall; Lieutenant Philip West, 32, of Budock Water, Cornwall; Lieutenant Marc Lawrence, 26, of Westgate-on-Sea, Kent; Lieutenant Andrew Wilson, 36, of Exeter and Lieutenant Thomas Mullen Adams, 27, of the US navy.*

⊷ For King and Country ⊶

*Army blacksmiths who served during the First World War.
Corporal Tom Eva on the right hand of the middle row in uniform. Many of the horses
shipped over from Canada were fine animals which unfortunately had
poorly-maintained feet which made them difficult to shoe.*

Armistice Day parade 1925.

✒ For King and Country ✒

Clockwise from above left: *Tom Eva as a raw recruit at the start of the First World War; A.H. Hawke in the Royal Flying Corps, 1917; William James Rowe with his sister during the First World War; Corporal Tom Eva mounted on his horse.*

Chapter 4: Life Between the Wars 1918–39

Harry Jenkin

My father Harry Jenkin came out of the Navy in 1908 as a widower with three daughters. He lived at 68 Meneage Street close to the James family and in 1909, aged 43, married my mother, Laura Lander James, aged 31. The couple had a second family, of four sons (myself being the third). Harry, born in 1912, was killed on his toy pedal car coming down Meneage Street near the Baptist Chapel (now the squash courts) when he fell out of the toy vehicle and struck his temple on a granite water spout. He died within 36 hours.

Many years later I was coming down Meneage Street on a bicycle when my brakes snapped. Father was standing outside the front door, smoking his pipe, and as I jumped off my bike to save myself, it continued down the hill and smashed into the back of a horse and cart. Had there been hard tarmac at that time I might have done myself a real injury but as it was I had only a few grazes on my leg. Father came across to me and calmly asked me if I was alright before telling me to go and fetch my bike and bring it to the top of the garden. There he proceeded to smash it to pieces with a sledge hammer, so distraught was he at such a vivid reminder of Harry's death which had happened not far away. For my own part I was not allowed to have another bike until I could afford to buy one myself.

The second son, John, was born on 12 July 1913 when my father was foreman of Sleeman's Brewery in Meneage Street. On the same site there was also a farm where we got our daily milk and cream on Sundays. In April 1913 with war looming Father had been recalled to the Colours and saw service at sea until 1916 when he was invalided out, having become Chief Petty Officer. He retired with a good pension, which he worked hard to supplement to support his large family – he appeared able to turn his hand to almost anything. At the time I was born at 98 Meneage Street, on 10 August 1916, he was 50, and working as an insurance aent. By the time of my brother Percy's birth, he was storeman at Trouson's Yard..

Father's training had made him a very strict disciplinarian and when he told us to do something there was never any argument. Despite being older and therefore less active than many fathers, he saw to it that we never wanted for anything; what we lost in one way, we gained in another. We always had a Sunday suit and boots to put on and food on the table which is more than could be said for of many our age. Father died on 1 April 1945, having by then received the Navy pension for longer than most (1907–1945).

One of the things which I remember as a boy was his special paraffin hand lamp which gave out a particularly good light; on a very dark night he would pick it up and take the three of us to the very of Beacon Barns Fields (which later became a housing development). From here there was a pathway leading out to Clodgey Lane and further out a group of allotments surrounded by very high Cornish stone hedges. Perched on a hedge, we would turn out the lamp and look at the night sky while father pointed out the different stars, made familiar to him from his years spent in the Navy. Eventually we would pick up the reflections of the Lizard Light and, standing up on a cloudless night, we could sometimes spot the St Anthony light, the Longships or, on rare occasions, the Godrevy. On the walk home we took turns to carry the wonderful paraffin lantern. We would stop at Lawrences, the fish and chip shop, to have a pennyworth of chips before heading home to light the candle before bed. That was a good night's entertainment. On one afternoon afternoon in 1927 we went up to the Downs to witness an eclipse of the sun. Just as the eclipse started a flock of swans came into view and so confused were they by the sudden darkness that they flew around in circles.

We had a walled garden at No. 68 where we kept chickens for eggs and for the table. Here father also had his workshop with a galvanised roof where he made his 'herbie beer'. We would go out collecting the ingredients for the delicious beer and, in particularly hot weather, it was not unusual to hear a mighty bang from the shed as another bottle of the stuff exploded in the heat!

Walking was one of our great pastimes – especially on the town's half day, Friday, when we headed out to the cove at Gunwalloe where we loved to fish (always unsuccessfully) in the pool using cotton and bent pins. The trip took us by way of Helston Downs, through Eglos Dairy and down through Content. We usually stopped at Mrs Lane's to fill up our bottles of water and then continued on down to the bottom of Tangies Hill where a well provided another chance for a drink.

During his time working for P.H. Tonkin, who had a business at the back of the present Museum,

Father took me on his rounds in a pony and trap buying hundreds of rabbits from the trappers and collecting eggs from the farms and smallholdings in the district. Back at the Tonkin premises he tested the eggs by holding them up against a lamp in a dark corner at the far end of the yard where there was also a room hung with rail upon rail of dead rabbits. Later they would be put into crates and and taken by my father up to Helston Station to join scores and scores of other crates from businesses throughout the district all waiting to be transported to London and Birmingham. Any pheasants collected on his rounds were a perk for my father and he would put them in a bag and take them straight over to the Angel. He had wonderful copper-plate handwriting, and all of the labels were beautifully written. As part of his work for P.H. Tonkin, he would take on an extra four or five men to collect, stack and pack rabbits for despatch during the height of the season, and I remember occasions when he came home unhappy with a man he had employed. He always blamed himself rather than that of the man in question, for according to my father the employer should always be able to suss a man out and discover his worth before taking him on.

In the days of my childhood, travel was severely limited and it was really only on the odd occasion – when my father borrowed the pony and trap from Mr Tonkin on a Sunday – that we could have a real day out to the beach. With us would come Aunt Emily and Grandma James, whose chair had to be lashed fast to the cart. Here she always sat, wearing a long, lace-trimmed black skirt with a rope tied around her and fastened to the chair like a modern safety belt. At Tangies Hill we had to get off to lighten the load as well as to give an occasional push in the very steep places.

HELSTON ROADS

In the early 1920s, the roads in Helston were made of earth (although long before this they may have been cobbled). In order to keep the dust down in the summer a man with a horse-drawn cart fitted with a water butt went around the town spraying the roads. He would start before the sun was up and continue throughout the day, regulating the flow from the sprinkler with a specially-fitted lever. Another man called Mr Kingdon (who lived in Martins Row) drove a steamroller, his job being to ensure that the road surface could not be washed away during bad winter weather. This he did by constantly pushing broken stone (grit) into the surface of the roads and compacting it with his roller.

When charabancs first arrived, there was only one in the area, an open-touring vehicle that belonged to Will's at Porthleven (*see page 141*). One evening in 1926 we went with the Church Street Guild on a mystery tour, to Kennack. The bus stopped at the top of the hill and we walked down to Kennack Sands and back again. On the return journey we were coming around Goonhilly when the bus broke down and we had no alternative but to walk singing hymns all the way home. As we came through Garras it was dark and those in their houses who heard the singing came out to see what on earth was going on. So ended my first trip in a charabanc. It had hard wheels, and I was nine or ten years old.

Meneage Street Methodist Bible Class, 1937. (Courtesy Sheila Stiddeford)
Left to right, back row: Phyllis Bassett, Elise Kiddicoat, Ev. Sillence, Olga Cardew, Noreena Williams, Joan Liddicoat, Mrs J.H. Thomas, Janie Crapp, ?, Janie Williams, Violet Wilcocks;
middle: Ken Thomas, Donald Thomas, Audrey Williams, Reg Liddicoat, Cecil Williams, Gordon Angove, Gladys Thomas, Millicent Cardew, Connie Roberts, Mr William Wear;
front: Arthur Sillence, Sylvie Cardew, ? Squib, ? Squib, Mr S. Sillence, L.W. Oliver, J.H. Thomas, J. Stideford, Margaret Stiddeford, Bert Williams, Florrie Williams, Vera Wilcocks.

Attending Chapel in Helston

Something which always puzzled me as a boy was the fact that Grandpa James would go down to Wesley with Uncle Fred and Aunt Annie whilst Uncle Ernie, Mother and the rest of my family went down to the United Methodist Chapel in Church Street. We would pass Auntie and Uncle Fred coming down Wendron Street, with Grandpa on our side. Grandpa would leave us and join them and go down Coinagehall Street while our group continued down Church Street. I believe that matters got to this stage after an argument between Uncle Fred, who was a builder, and Uncle Ernie, who was a carpenter, and who may have been in partnership together at one stage.

The chapels in those days were a central part of everyday life; there was little else for entertainment – no radio, no television, no electric light, and most things centred around Chapel. At Church Street we had the Guild which met on Thurday nights, and we often put on plays down in the school room which we then took on tour in the locality. At this time the Brays, a great chapel family, owned a business in Church Street and had a motorised van in which we transported all of our scenery, whilst the cast made their way around on bicycles.

The Sunday School Anniversay was one of the highlights of the year. At 2.15p.m. on the given Sunday the chapel would be filled to bursting and one had to arrive early to get a seat. Members of the Sunday School assembled down in the school room and walked up through the chapel to take their places, smiling at everybody en-route. On one occasion I had to say my piece in the pulpit whilst standing precariously on a chair as I was so small. Clinging to the gas pipe to stop myself from falling, I fluffed my lines and had to be prompted by Mr Edward Cunnack who was sitting in the seat behind. I had a little blue silk suit on, and he pinched my bottom and whispered my lines to me as I forgot each and every one.

On the Friday after this celebration day we always went on an outing to Carbis Bay with the Sunday School teachers, the superintendents, Mr Cunnack, Mr Rowse and Mr Courtier, and the mothers. This was the only time of the year that we travelled by train and it was widely regarded as the best event of the year. The train went straight through without changing at Gwinear Road or St Erth and there was always great excitement up on the platform. The Wesleyan Sunday School went on the same train, but we never got together – we would go in at the bottom end and they would go in at the top end. Similarly, at the beach we would keep to our separate ends of the bay. If I had two shillings to spend on a Sunday School tea treat I would come back with money in my pocket; donkey rides were only one penny given by a man called Payne who used to keep the donkeys and control the beach. In the afternoon we walked into St Ives along the footpath parallel to the railway line, then walked back again and at 4p.m. were given saffron buns and tea before races and games.

Church Street Chapel Sunday School outing to Carbis Bay, c.1926.
Left to right: Clarence Ould, Bill Rogers, Lionel Rogers, Harry Hitchens and Ernie Moyle.

St Mary's Roman Catholic Church.

Church of Jesus Christ of the Latter Day Saints, often referred to as the Mormon church and the Helston Family History Centre.

*Helston Council School Football Team, 1928/9.
Left to right, back: Dick Rawlings, Charlie Uren, Jack Channon (behind), Lionel Rogers (in front), Jack Williams, Reg Jenkin;
front: Mr Thomas Hart, Clarence Ould, Harry Symons, Bill Rogers, Tom Downing, Cyril Reed.*

National School for Boys, 1920s.

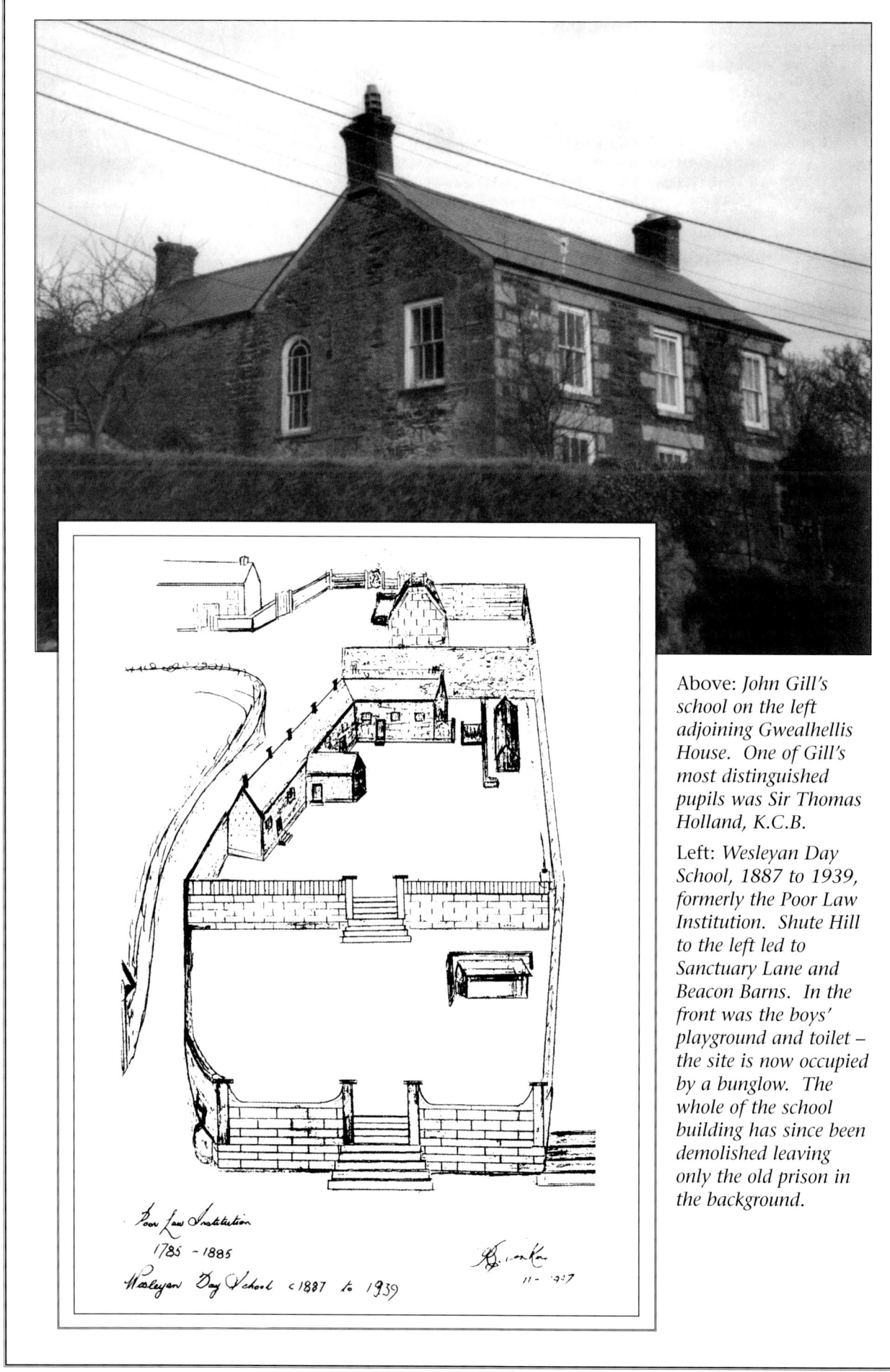

Above: *John Gill's school on the left adjoining Gwealhellis House. One of Gill's most distinguished pupils was Sir Thomas Holland, K.C.B.*

Left: *Wesleyan Day School, 1887 to 1939, formerly the Poor Law Institution. Shute Hill to the left led to Sanctuary Lane and Beacon Barns. In the front was the boys' playground and toilet – the site is now occupied by a bunglow. The whole of the school building has since been demolished leaving only the old prison in the background.*

SCHOOLDAYS

There were three schools in Helston when I began my education; Helston County School, the Church School over in Church Street (known also as the National School) and the Wesleyan Day School. As a boy I went to the latter, which was up on Shute Hill, and was built as a workhouse in 1755. It later became a Union taking in people from Helston and the surrounding areas. This Union lasted for 100 years until 1855, when Meneage Hospital was built and to which the incumbents were transferred. In about 1858 the Wesleyans bought the old Union building and made it into a school.

The windows were so high that nobody could look out of them and the partitions were made of glass so one could hear what was going on in the next room. The teachers were Mr Hart, Miss May Winn, Miss Annie Moyle, Mrs Oliver and Mrs Eddy. All were very strict, especially Mr Hart who had control over the running of the school. If we saw our teachers out of school hours we treated them with great respect, raising our caps and saying 'Good morning Mr Hart', or 'Good afternoon Mrs Oliver'.

The building itself was an unpleasant place and should never have been used for the education of children. Cold water ran from taps into a long granite trough for washing one's hands and the toilets were earthen closets in the lower playground. The only heating we had was a small tortoise coke stove in one corner of the room; during the winter it was bitterly cold.

One of my most unpleasant memories of school was the eleven-plus exam, which every student had to take. I can still see Mr Hart now, standing up in front of the class when the results came through. He held up a list of the class and said:

'As you can see there is a line going across, those above the line will be going to the Grammar School, those below the line haven't failed, but there isn't room for you [there]'.

Above: *The three teachers at Trannack, c.1923: Mr Perkins Coles with Miss Gwendoline James behind and Miss Knight to her right.*
Below: *Helston County School staff, 1910. Included are Mr Haydon, Miss Baldwin, Miss Jacobi, Miss Sumerling, Miss McDowell, Miss Cannan, Mr Cooper, Mr Boxhall and Mr Baines.*

All of the other children were fee-paying and mine was one of the names under the line. With my parents unable to pay for me to go to the Grammar School, I stayed where I was until the age of 14, being taught by Mr Hart who, despite being strict, was fair.

Mr E.G. Curtis who lived in Station Road and kept the grocers before Trounsons arrived, once came to school with Miss Rows, a school governor. He wanted a composition written on 'The League of Nations' and offered prizes for the best essays; 2s.6d. for the best overall, 2 shillings for the second best and 1s.6d. for third. I made a great effort to win myself a prize and enlisted the help of my parents in the task. I wrote down everything I could find out and finished off by saying 'Beneath the rule of men so entirely great, the pen is mightier than the sword'. Mr Curtis was very impressed and I won first prize. Where I got the saying from I have no idea, but I must have read it somewhere and then copied it out word for word.

We had no real playground to play in at school although during my last two years there we acquired a games field out towards Clodgey Lane. Before we could play on it however we had to go out and pick up the cow pats and then rig up our own goal posts with whatever came to hand. After I left in 1930 the school did develop both a football and a cricket team of its own.

Helston Male Voice Choir, 1938/9. Left to right, back: ?, ? Jones, Robert Bassett, George Hooper, ? Endean, Arthur Reed, ?, Bill Streng, Jack Johns; centre: Bill Wear, Percy Liddicoat, George Pascoe, Jonnie Williams, Billy Rowe, Norman Treloar, ? Rogers, Jack Broadhurst, ?, Ernie Guiton, Reggie Bowden; front: Bert Williams, Smacker Rowe, John James, Maurice Williams, Willie Pascoe, Jim Opie (conductor), Ginger Rowe, ? Manning, Tom Pollard, John Richards, Wilfred Bassett.

Wesleyan Day School, 1924/5. Left to right, back: Lionel Symons, Jack Nancollis, W. Bowden, Harry Curtis, Olwyn Williams, Reg Moyle; middle: ?, George Pascoe, Gwen Pascoe, Martha Treloar, ?, H. Curnow, Phyllis Charles, M. Jory, ?, ?; front: P. Bowden, John Jenkin, L. Pascoe (?), Harry Symons, Dick Rawlings, Tommy Downing, Bill Rogers, ?, Henry Choak.

My First Job

When I was ten years old Father came home one day and said 'Son, I've got a job for you, come with me.' I followed him down the street, not knowing where we were going until we arrived at Joe Pascoe's Shoe Shop and Father said 'Here he is, see what you can do by him.' In those days people in the trade had a leather strop for putting the final cutting edge on their sharp knives and Joe Pascoe picked up his strop, flexed it and declared 'Any nonsense and you'll get this across your backside.' I stayed there for four years.

I began work at 8a.m. sweeping up the shop and getting everything ready for the four cobblers who began to arrive at half-past. I then went to school and would return at 4p.m. and stay until 6p.m. labelling boots and shoes or taking repaired items back to customers throughout the town, some of whom gave me a penny and others a bun. On Saturdays, I started at 8a.m. and finished at 9p.m. Saturday was a very busy day and I remember that I had to write labels, such as 'Morcomb Sworne, soled and heeled'; I never saw the man, just his boots, and had all the farmers' names stuck in my mind. One that seemed particularly unusual to me was Curnow Condurrow; for years I didn't realise that the name included the address!

Instead of 'soled and heeled', I once wrote 'sold and helled' by mistake – an incident I was not allowed to forget in a hurry. I would come into the shop and be greeted with 'Here's that sold and helled man come again'.

I earned 2 shillings a week to start with and gradually this crept up to 2s.6d. – all of which I gave to Mother who gave me back sixpence on Friday nights for a pomegranate or a pennyworth of sweets from Miss Oates' shop up Wendron Street followed by a trip to the pictures for tuppence. They were silent films back then and Bert James would be in there thumping the piano. We would be up to our knees in peanut shells and if things weren't going right we used to flick the shells at the screen from the front row where we always sat (these being the cheapest seats). As the horses galloped across the screen so Bert would rattle faster and faster along on the piano. When we came out we would go to the chip shop for a pennyworth of chips and then head home having spent four or five pence leaving only a penny or two for the rest of the week.

Bert James was Uncle Ernie's son and lived above Reed's seed shop in Meneage Street, where Kays is now. They subsequently moved out of there they went to live at 73 Meneage Street in a flat above the present-day picture framers.

Town Time

Electricity arrived at our home in 1929 and to begin with we had three lights fitted for £2.5s. Our next-door neighbour, who was a motor mechanic, extended our lights upstairs after the electricity board had finished. And how terrific it was to be able to go to bed without a candle!

With no radio it was very difficult to tell the time; the chiming of the town clock was hard to make out unless the wind was blowing in the right direction and everybody's watch seemed to be either fast or slow, so that when one asked a person the time, they would take out their watch and say 'It is about 4 o'clock', never giving an accurate answer for fear of being wrong. When we had radio we all went by radio time and people could check their watches at last. The train left Helston at 11.55a.m., so Mother used to make use of the train sounding its whistle to keep her own time check on the morning. Another time-keeper was an old chap called Joe Johns who walked in every day from Lowertown to work at John Toy's Foundry. He would go in each morning at 6.55a.m. carrying his lantern and Mother would wake us as she heard his hob-nailed boots clattering on the pavement. If anybody wanted an early call Mr Johns would knock on their door and wake them up on his way to work.

Another familiar sound was the Lizard foghorn – a sure sign of a change in the weather. We also listened to the kennels running down the side of Meneage Street; amidst the relative silence it was like music to us as we lay in bed at night. In the distance we also occasionally heard the Loe Bar moaning and the blasting at the quarries.

TOY & CO.,

Proprietors - J. LUKE, R.V. LUKE

IRON AND BRASS FOUNDERS

ENGINEERS AND PLUMBERS

Meneage Street, Helston.

Makers of all kinds of Cooking Ranges, fitted with Welded Steel Boilers for Hot and cold Water Services to Baths, Lavatories, etc.
Electric Bell Installations. Water Closets.
Hydraulic Rams and Hand Pumps.
Water Wheels fitted with Force Pumps.
Repairs to all kinds of Farm Implements and Machinery.
Lawn Mowers Repaired & Machine Ground.
New Parts supplied.
Orders from Town or Country receive prompt attention
Buyers of Scrap Iron, Copper, Brass and Lead.

Toy's was one of three smithies in Meneage Street; there was also one up in Clies Yard run by Mr Oates, and one at the top of town where Joe Gainey worked for many years. After the Second World War this was taken on by Mr Faull.

Saturdays in Helston

Throughout the 1920s, Saturday nights in Helston were a festive affair. Every pub had its own stabling so each place would fill up quickly with horses and traps – close to us we had the Rodney Yard, Meneage Yard and Cade's Yard. On Saturdays all of the shops stayed open until at least 9p.m. and grocers such as Trounson's would busy themselves with delivering the farmers' groceries to the traps stood ready outside the pubs. Whoever was in charge of the yard would put the goods in the trap and make sure that they were taken home.

The Salvation Army band played outside Miss Lugg's shop from 7p.m. to 8p.m. and then they would go down and play on the cobbles outside Lloyds Bank for the next hour. When the buses left for the outlying villages at 10.10p.m. it was impossible to move for the crush. All made their last stop outside our house and they were so crowded after coming from the station and the other areas of town that people used to have to lie on top of the vehicles and hold on to the ladders at the back. It was all very friendly, however, and there was certainly no vandalism.

The streets at that time were lit by gas and it was the task of a Mr Dan Scholar to travel around with a pole, at the top of which was a hook and a sheath with a candle inside. The hook was used to turn on the gas supply, while the sheath was lowered and the gas lit, all in one operation. A favourite joke was to shin up the lampost and turn them off again!

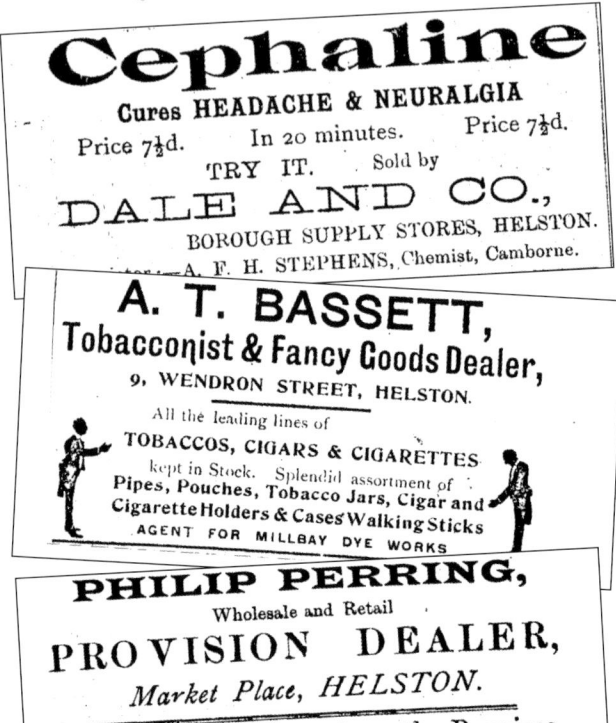

Funerals in Helston

One day in 1933, during my time with St John's Ambulance, we were called down to an old lodging house in the town run by a man called Tossell, who I remember had a gold ring in one of his ears. Mr Tossell ran a lodging house for people with limited financial resources, but who didn't want to go to the Workhouse. We picked him up and took him up to the Cottage Hospital and that, as far as I was concerned, was the end of the matter. However, one evening Uncle Ernie paid one of his visits to enquire whether any of us would like to accompany him for a walk. I accepted and when we got up to the hospital, he told me that he had to go in to speak with the matron. He knocked on the door, one of the girls opened it and we entered to see Miss Sergeant standing in the hallway. She said 'Oh Mr James, you know where to go', to which Uncle Ernie replied that he did and headed off in the direction of the mortuary. Here we found Mr Tossell laid out and we measured him for his coffin. It was the first time that I had seen a corpse, it scared the living daylights out of me and I didn't sleep all night.

Helston undertakers were also carpenters by profession and they were many in number, including Winn's, Mac Trezise and the Martin Brothers. Winn's carpenters was at St Johns up the old road, Mac Trezise's was up Meneage Street in Prospect Place, whilst the Martin brothers were on the site of what is now Furry Way. There were also several carpenters who operated one-man businesses.

At the bottom of Shute Hill there was a building on the left which housed Peter James' horse-drawn hearse. Peter was the father of Edwin James who had the bakers and Arthur James who had the pork shop, and he used to hire out the hearse to the various undertakers in town. For each funeral Peter James would hitch up the horse and take the hearse to the home of the deceased. Everybody would gather outside the house and walk behind the procession to the cemetery – except for the direct mourners who sometimes travelled instead by horse and carriage. Funerals generally took place on a Sunday afternoon because people could not afford to lose valuable work time.

Work at the Haberdashers

When I left school there was no work and my parents were certainly concerned as to what opportunity might be open to me. Aged 14 at the time, I had not decided what direction I wanted to take and so had little choice in the matter when a job was accepted for me at the outfitting shop in Market Place. The shop was run on the site where Bowdens is now and the proprietor was a Mr Hebden Coombes.

Gradually the business turned increasingly towards drapery and ladies' fashionwear but to start off with my job was restricted to the role of tea-boy and I also had to clean up the shop and see to it that the stock was neat and tidy. There were three of us, and we each had a stock room to look after. Most of it had been left there by the former owner, Mr W.J. Hosking, and was nearly all relatively old so had to be solf off as fast as possible. I had to look after the area where the corduroy trousers were stored, together with the odd waistcoats. Every week they were taken out and sorted according to size, shaken, folded and put back in their proper places ready for next week's business.

I never enjoyed going to work as the place seemed depressing and it was almost as if I had been forced into the job. Mr Coombes was a nice man and a good employer but the wages, at 4 shillings a week at the age of 18 didn't permit a lavish lifestyle. Inevitably Sundays were something to look forward to. We worked through until 9p.m. on Saturdays, but also had Friday afternoons off, when I would get out the bike and go 'beaching' or up to the Downs with other boys to play cricket.

After four years I had finally served my apprenticeship as a drapery assistant and Mr Coombes would not keep me on because at 18 he could not afford to pay me. He suggested that he write off to Cook, Son & Co at 22 St Paul's Churchyard and ask if they would take me on. This he did and so off I went to London for an interview. A trip to London in those days was like travelling to the ends of the earth, so my sister Erna came with me and we stayed out with my mother's sister, Aunt Katie, for a couple of days at Ferntower Road, Highbury.

Moving to London was also something which my mother's brother, Willie James, had done, and it was perhaps because she thought that I might follow in his footsteps that I was encouraged to go. Uncle Willie served his apprenticeship with the Helston firm, B. Thomas, as a tailor and outfitter and then went to work at Jeremiah Rotheram's in Shoreditch. He did very well there, finishing up as a buyer in one of the departments. Sadly he died early in life.

Slaughterhouses and The Leather Industry

Mr Arthur James, the pork butcher, used to kill his pigs at the bottom of Shute Hill which takes its name from the water shute. Leslie Spargo had a killing house in Meneage Street and Charlie Oliver also ran a similar establishment at the top of Meneage Road. Other slaughterhouse owners included E.C. Oliver, whose premises were in Bullock Lane, Mr Hawke, who had a killing house at the bottom of town, and Cunnack's on the Moors. Mr Dale at Gunwalloe killed his own beef, as did Eastmans.

In my youth the killing of an animal was a most inhumane event involving a pole axe and a nasty blow to the head. I witnessed the killing of an animal just once and that was enough for me. Soon after this the humane killers were introduced. Cattle in those days were starved for 24 hours before slaughtering but, unlike today's era of crowded lorries and long journeys, they were at least brought to their deaths in a calm and unstressed state.

Helston was the centre of an active leather industry. There were several saddlers who made harnesses, saddles, bridles, bits, whips, etc. as well as the great many boot and shoe makers of the town. And, as has already been mentioned, leather was also used to make the valves in the water pumps.

At Holland's Mill, oak bark was crushed to produce the tannin for treating the hides taken from locally killed cattle and horses, particularly from Cunnack's Tannery in Tanyard Lane (of which a full, illustrated description of the process can be found in the companion title *The Book of Grampound with Creed*). There were drying rooms in Meneage Street at the back of what is now Oliver's butcher's shop and which was once Mr Cunnack's office next door to the family home. Here the louvered vents can still be seen inside the building although they have been sealed up.

Territorial Army, August 1939. Local members were called to camp at Arne Heath, Wareham, Dorset. Left to right, back: ? James, ? Bond, ?, ?, ? Stephen, ? Orchard, ? Stephen, Jack Downs, Cyril Reed; 3rd row: ? Dykes, ? Penulula, ?, J. Kemp, ? Pascoe, Chas Wearne, ?, ?; 2nd row: George Hart, Ed Harris, ? Roberts, John Dower, ? Pascoe, L. Sharp, D.L. Gilbert, Harry Pascoe, Cyril Stevens; front: Percy Pethick, ? Lawson, Sgt G. Short, Lt George Berriman, Major Polglaze, Sgt English, ?, T.L. Oliver, ?, ? Williams.

Helston ARP (civil defence force), 1944. Left to right, back: John Blee, Bert Lugg, Hartly Peters, Stephen Eva, A. Thorner, Gordon Bray, Headly Julian, middle: Ben Treloar, Joe Rowe, ? Bassett, Harry Martin, Joe Watters, Dick Reed, Percy Williams, Doug Curtis, Len Pascoe front: Henry Prisk, ? Hall, Dick Jennings, Gordon Kneebone, Williams Trezise, Dick Laity, Bert Badcock, Ray Goodhead, Clifford Bray.

Chapter 5: The Second World War 1939–45

THE APPROACH OF WAR

At the age of 18 I went to London for a job interview with a Helston man called Mr Oates. He had been to school with my father, had a sister, Mrs Diamond, who lived in Godolphin Road and also had other relations who kept a fruit shop in Wendron Street. As Director of Cook, Son & Co. he had done well. He was very interested in me and saw to it that I had one or two privileges. He asked me what I wanted to do and I explained that I wasn't really interested in the drapery line at all, that I wasn't a good sales person and that I wanted to use my hands like my brother John who was in the painting and decorating trade. Mr Oates was very sypathetic to my case and although unable to do anything for me immediately suggested that I might later move into the design department where all the stands were made for the external shows.

After about eight months, true to his word, Mr Oates saw to it that I was given a job with the advertising and design department. Situated next door to St Paul's Cathedral, Cook, Son & Co. sold anything and everything and employed a staff of over 3000. In my new role, I took up painting and a bit of carpentry and made stands which were then taken to the various fairs where the company displayed their wares. From 1936–39, I truly enjoyed my job for the first time.

Then the war came! I volunteered for the RAF just after the outbreak of war, but was not called up until January 1940. After my intial training, I had a spell at Calshot before embarking for France in early 1940. At Cherbourg we unloaded the boats and in their place took on board ship the injured to be brought back home. Despite being in the RAF I had not seen an aeroplane since leaving the flying boat at Calshot (which even then I had had nothing to do with). This experience was not uncommon, for in the early stages of the war there was such a great deal to organise that planes were, for a while, in relatively short supply.

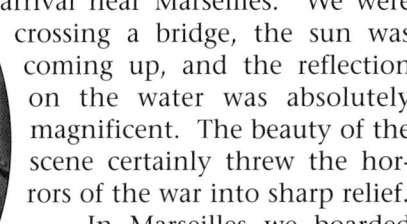

The three Jenkin boys during the Second World War. Clockwise from top: Reg, John, Percy.

In Cherbourg we were bombed and straffed and eventually were moved south. We went by lorry to Paris as far as I can recall, and then by train from Paris to Marseilles. On this leg of the journey we were warned not to buy anything during stops for refuelling, etc. Unfortunately some of the lads ignored this rule and bought bottles of wine and some food. As a result, a number were lost through drinking poisoned goods. Needless to say, it was not a very pleasant journey and we lived on biscuits and tins of McConnich's meat and vegetable soup. Water was our only drink. I will never forget the early morning of our arrival near Marseilles. We were crossing a bridge, the sun was coming up, and the reflection on the water was absolutely magnificent. The beauty of the scene certainly threw the horrors of the war into sharp relief.

In Marseilles we boarded the troopship HMS *Devonshire* which, though designed to carry 3000 men, had 6000 on board. As we headed west we could see the Rock of Gibraltar, from which point, stretching towards Africa, was a rainbow which we seemed to sail through as we dropped anchor off the coast. Here we stayed for several days before turning and heading eastwards. Nobody knew where we were going, or what we were going to be asked to do. The next stop was Valetta Harbour, Malta, where we picked up water, food and other provisions. Then we went on, without a clue of our destination, but ended up in Alexandria. With no real place for sleeping and eating, everyone had to make do and I slept in a big box intended for lifebuoys. This resting place was to prove my bed for an entire fortnight and once again the cold tins of McConnich's soup provided the only food on board!

After a journey where we had felt more like herded animals than servicemen, we arrived on the Alexandria quayside to receive a severe dressing down from the Warrant Officer for not looking airmanlike! Having invited questions, the WO was asked by one of the chaps how long we were likely to be there. The answer was very simple:

Friends Near and Far

A meeting of seven Helston boys in Cairo, 1942. Left to right: A.V. Bassett, R. Phillips, W. Rogers, R. Bassett, R. Jenkin, S. Bassett, J. Jenkin.

A street party in Jubilee Terrace, Helston, put on to celebrate the coronation of Queen Elizabeth II, 1953.

THE SECOND WORLD WAR

As long as the war takes. Those of you that are married, you'll be here for at least three years and those of you who are not married will be here for at least four years.

It felt like a prison sentence – especially at such a young age. There was no way of getting home, and no break from the work apart from local leave. I was extremely lucky in that I was attached to Headquarters Middle East and was therefore stationed at a big RAF base called Heliopolis (City of the Sun) where life was considerably better than it might otherwise have been.

As it turned out, I was indeed in Egypt for over four years. One of the worst experiences during that time was a spell of sand-fly fever; I was shaking all over, they took me to hospital and there I stayed for five weeks. One day during my illness the Flight Sergeant came in and informed me that the Padre was on his way in to see me, at which piece of information I assumed that my condition must have been more serious that I had thought! The Padre was very nice and came in to tell me that I was able to go on sick leave to a pleasant place in Tel Aviv in Palestine. 'If there's anything you want', he explained, 'tell me and I'll try to get it for you.' When he returned I told him that having been in hospital for five weeks I did not have any money and he arranged for the Pay Officer to come along and sort out the problem. On that particular day several editions of the *West Briton* arrived for me from Helston – they always came in a bundle of five or six at once. Whilst reading them I fell sleep and found, on waking, the Flight Lieutenant reading the papers. Before the war he was an accountant who was employed by Simpsons the outfitters of Penzance and Helston. He fixed me up with the money I wanted and after that I made a point of passing on the occasional *West Briton* to him once I had finished with it.

One day I had a letter from Father telling me that living in Cairo was a Doctor Dale who, if I was ever in the city, I should look up and introduce myself. I found out his address in the phone book and one day went in to see him. His parents ran the drapers in Coinagehall Street which later became Oxenhams. He had lost a leg in Galipoli and was by that time the British Embassy doctor in Cairo. He made me very welcome and when I told him that there were other Helston boys in the area he decided that he wanted to see them all. He became a great friend and always left a meal for us. I used to phone up and tell him there were five or six or more coming over and he would say 'OK all come along and have a nice meal. I shall be there later.' He also left cinema tickets for us. All in all there were seven or eight Helston lads from the three services who met up from time to time, including Vincent from Porthleven, three Bassetts from Helston, brother John and myself. John was involved in the siege of Tobruk (14 April – 7 December 1941) and during his time in hospital in Alexandria I went to see him. After the war when Nasser (later President of Egypt) came along, Doctor Dale returned to Helston virtually penniless.

I went to Malta once, but in letters home we were forbidden to let slip anything of our whereabouts so I dropped hints instead, writing 'I do miss my Maltesers and I would like you to send on a few packets.' At home, however, the penny didn't drop as to my whereabouts and months later a food parcel packed with Maltesers finally caught up with me after being posted on numerous times.

When I knew that my brother John had finished his stint in Egypt and that he was on the list to go home, I forewarned my family of the good news in code. When sending a message home we were allowed to do so using a standard lettergram, picking numbers which offered a choice of sentences. I sent the message 'I hope John has a nice leave' and they twigged that he was finally on his way home.

Edgar Hawke at War with the DCLI (Duke of Cornwall Light Infantry) in the Middle East.

News from Back Home

Like many of the men I joined up with, my own father had been lucky enough to return from the First World War. 'A war to end all wars' it certainly had not turned out to be and we all hoped that 'our war' would be all over as quickly as possible so that life could return to normal. Whilst away what was important to me, and to many of the men that I was with, was to try to keep in touch with what was happening at home. I was fortunate in that I had a supply of the *West Briton* which readily supplemented the letters from home. The latter kept me informed as to what was happening to the family – in particular to my brother Percy who was in the Navy – and I had occasional contact with John who was serving in the Army in Egypt.

I had had first-hand experience of the war in France, but didn't return home until just before D-Day. I heard about the ARP (later the Civil Defence), the Home Guard and the Special Constables, as well as the various fund-raising activities such as War Weapons Week and the Wesleyan Church Canteen with its wonderful group of helpers, meeting the needs of servicemen in the home area. I did not hear about the bombs that fell down at St Johns until I returned home as this kind of event was not reported (although we did hear about the bombing of Falmouth).

Papers reported the removal of many of the metal railings to help in the war effort, including those around the Grylls Monument. It was good to hear that the children were still being encouraged to learn the Furry Dance despite the war, and that the tradition of 8 May was in essence being kept alive. The Grammar School, which in the early stages of the war shared its facilities with a school from West Ham, later appeared to be working much as normal. There were regular football and hockey matches and the annual Sport's Day still had its place.

Left: *Local trainee soldiers, Second World War.*

Right: *Helston Home Guard, 1945.*

Left: *Meeting of Cornishmen in Cairo, January 1943.*
Left to right, back: R. Jenkin, S. Bassett, S. Wheeler, A.V. Bassett, J. Jenkin, L. Thomas (Gweek); front: R. Bassett, W. Reardon (Penzance), W. Rogers.
This photograph was taken on a visit to Dr Dale, an ex-Helston man, who was working at the British Embassy.

Right: *In August 1941 President Roosevelt and Prime Minister Churchill met at sea off the Newfoundland coast and conceived the Atlantic Charter committing themselves to creating a world order in which democratic nations would unite to quash aggression and maintain the peace. Sir Winston crossed the Atlantic on HMS* Prince of Wales. *Percy Jenkin was on one of the mine-sweeping escort vessels and later received this signed photograph as a record of being on the scene for this secret meeting.*

BACK TO BLIGHTY

I returned to Britain in April 1944, just before D-Day, after four years and four months away. At the time of D-Day I was at Longleat Estate near Bath where the RAF had a great many buildings under the trees. In one of them we worked long hours decanting endless different colours of paint to be sent to different RAF bases for the painting of their gliders and planes. Every squadron had a different colour and we had to decant thousands and thousands of gallons of the stuff.

At Longleat we had a Group Captain who sent men out to sweep up the leaves whenever they fell from the trees onto the parade ground. I got so fed up with it that I went to see the Adjutant and requested a posting. He told me that they were after volunteers and that there were several places that I could go. I asked for whatever came first and this turned out to be Norway.

From Longleat we went up to Scotland and did a survival course in the mountains. Then we travelled down to Turnhouse for a glider training course (although why we did so remains a mystery as gliders were of no use in Norway). We then went to the coast and practised landings with a flotilla of boats. Time and time again we would go out to sea and come back and land – the practice went for weeks on end. After this they sent us back up into the mountains again.

Finally, at the end of April 1945, we went down to the coast and boarded a craft for Norway. Out in the North Sea we were blown all over the place by a severe gale, eventually coming safely into Stavanger on 1 May. There was no sign of any Germans, although there were occasional shots in the mountains. We stayed there for three days, before re-boarding our ships and going around the coast to Oslo where we arrived on 8 May. This of course was VE Day and for the Norwegians it was like being let out of prison. The suppression under German occupation had been terrible, and the celebrations were something to behold. I joined in to the full, thinking of the Flora Day celebrations back home and hearing in my mind the music of the Helston Band. I never forgot it. Other Helston men have said the same thing – a Helstonian called Mr Sampson, for example, said that on 8 May 1940 he heard the Helston Band playing before the guns began as the Germans laid down the barrage at the start of their Western Offensive. He always said that his war started on Flora Day 1940, and ended on Flora Day 1945!

Wartime Special Constables, 1945.
Left to right, back (surnames only available): ?, ?, ?, Martin, ?, ?, Bolitho, Hart, ?, Kneebone, ?, ?; centre: ?, Wimbledon, C.C. Martin, Beake, G. Haynes, L. Spargo, H. Symons, Symons, Pascoe, F. Courtis, L. Martin, ?, J. Waters; front: P. Stephens, C. Hyde, S. Wearne, ?, Sgt Stone, ?, ?, ?, ?, C. Williams, Pascoe, Pascoe, ?.

Meeting My Future Wife.

I remained in Norway from May 1945 until the following Christmas and during that time met the girl who was to become my wife, Inger. She had spent her teenage years under German occupation – a very unpleasant experience which even now she never talks about.

During the war her father operated a radio transmitter and receiver, whilst Inger worked for the resistance in quite a different capacity. Neither of them ever knew what the other was doing, although they were living in the same house and both working for the same organisation. Resistance workers were grouped into cells of three and no more which ensured that in the event of capture no single person could supply information on members of other cells. Inger worked in the Government building where all of the food coupons were printed; these she aquired and brought out of the building rolled up in a paper which was then taken from her by an unknown person on her way home by train. She never saw who took the papers from her; all she knew was that they took them to give to the underground.

I married Inger in Norway in November 1945 and she returned with me to live in England. Along with several other couples who had also married in Norway, we took an old, barely seaworthy German vessel and travelled back to Britain. The route we took was far from direct and we travelled right around the Orkney Islands where the rudder jammed leaving us to sail hopelessly in ever-decreasing circles for three days before finally coming into Liverpool. It was not a nice trip, but back at home Inger was at last introduced to the family. Word went around Helston that Reggie had married a foreigner which, in those days, was rather frowned upon – most would have said, 'what's wrong with good Cornish girls?!' However, Inger's English was quite competent and she could converse very comfortably with all the new people she met.

After my disembarkation leave was up, Inger stayed with mother and I went back to Leighton Buzzard where I remained until June 1946. During my six-and-a-half years of service I received not a single day's privilege leave, only embarkation, disembarkation and sick leave. When I went for my discharge on my demob at Leighton Buzzard, Group Captain Port told me that he thought I should remain in the RAF. 'No, I don't think so, ' I replied, 'do you realise I've not had one single day's leave in six-and-a-half years' service?' 'Neither,' he replied, 'did prisoners of war' and that was that. I was given my new grey pin-stripe suit, raincoat, shoes, shirt and tie, and a hat which was really a case of Hobson's choice – if it fitted, you took it. The clothes came in very useful and I also received a gratuity of £85 for my service.

Reggie and Inger's wedding in Norway, 1945. Best Man was Corporal Les Stacey and the Maid of Honour was Greth Haghan.

Mawgan Football Club, 1948/9.

Helston Town Band, 1955. Left to right, back row: I. Harvey, P. Goldsworthy, S. Wearne, S. Donning, C. Busby, N. Faulkner, K. Johns, D. Retallick, G. Pascoe; middle: R. Harvey, P. Bennets, M. Williams, M. Pascoe, F. Bell, L. Williams, M. Smith, L. Thorns, L. Ashton; front: M. Rosewarne, D. Townsend, K. Johns, K. Busby, E. Ashton, E. Pascoe, K. Roberts, C. Warrington, K. Meagor.

Chapter 6: Post-War Helston 1945–99

BACK TO CIVVY STREET

When I left the RAF I was entitled to the job which I had left behind, but we three brother had a tenuous understanding that we would go into the painting and decorating business together and hopefully all become partners, so Percy and I came back to Helston to join John. As it was, Percy went back up to Hartlepool with his wife where her parents had a ship's chandlers which supplied a wide variety of goods to the ships coming into the harbour – from food to mechanical parts. One Russian ship even wanted a piano and Percy scouted around the area for a good second-hand instrument which they dutifully supplied. He did well there and his move proved a wise choice.

Meanwhile, the painting and decorating got off to a good start because throughout the war years there had been very little decorating done, leaving an ideal opportunity in the market for our firm. On one occasion we even had 11 men working for us.

Inger and I lived with my mother for a time, and then moved to live above Miss Winn's Shop. Suzanne was born in 1947 in a nursing home in Greenlanes, Redruth. There was no petrol in those days and public transport was scarce. One Sunday night during Inger's 10-day stay in the nursing home, I was on my way walking to Redruth when a car passed me having come up from Turnpike. I could see who the man was and flagged him down, but he kept going. The British Legion had placed a great emphasis on helping ex-servicemen and I was wearing my RAF greatcoat, but nonetheless this man passed me by. I walked all the way to Redruth and no other vehicle came along the road. When I got there, the same man came out of the nursing home, jumped in his car and drove back to Helston again. Needless to say I had to walk all the way home again.

I was working out at Poldhu Cove in a house called Trewoon, for a Miss Trelawney who wanted to sell up to go to America. She asked me if I knew of anybody who would be willing to go and live there for one or two years until the place was sold and I went and talked it over with Inger. We decided to go out there to live, from early Easter until the Autumn. We looked after the chickens which Miss Trelawney had left behind, eating the eggs as they were produced. It was wonderful for Inger and baby Suzanne; they spent many happy days in the open air and from Trewoon I cycled to and from work. Eventually the place was sold up and in the autumn of 1947 we moved back to Helston to the new Cornish Unit house, where we still live. This group of ten houses was built before the through road (Trengrouse Way) was cut right through to Clodgey Lane and the inhabitants were nearly all ex-servicemen; Stanley Oates, the jeweller, lived opposite, and Laurie Pascoe was our immediate neighbour. The only non-serviceman was the town surveyor, who lived in the end house up there. With our house the last to be finished, we were also the last to move in. Our son John was born in the house thwo years later.

The Cornish units were relatively cheap and quick to erect, but they were cold, draughty and miserable. When they were built they were intended to last 20 to 25 years after which time the tops would be taken off and the dwellings turned into bungalows. As it turned out, however, the bottoms gave out before the tops. Everything was pre-fabricated and the components were made of dis-used china clay, with cement mixed in. The cement mixture was moulded into different patterns, which all slotted together to form the lower walls. The upper storey was timber framed and built on site with tiles hung on the outside.

Literally thousands of these houses were built throughout the UK and when, some 40 years later, the steel which had been used to reinforce the uprights began to rust and the Government decided to get the houses re-furbished, little did they realise just how many there were to be done. Some, including the Culdrose units, have never been tackled. Work began on our house in 1990 and the contractors knocked down all of the ground-floor walls. The only things left standing on the ground floor were the stairs and the chimney. The building was supported on props and they took away everything of the lower walls and then rebuilt all of the external walls upwards, gradually lowering the props to allow the upper storey to settle on the newly-built lower storey. Thermalite insulation blocks were used on the inside, the cavity was filled with foam, and stone-faced concrete blocks were used on the outside. Windows with modern double-glazed units replaced the original intallations and the result is that we now have a warm, energy-efficient home.

The Jenkin Family

The Jenkin family, 1940. This photograph was taken to send to the three sons who were serving in the forces. Included are Joan (John's Wife), Erna, Anne (John's first daughter), Mr S.H. Jenkin and Laura (Mother).

*The Jenkin family at St Ives, 1950.
Left to right, back: Laura, Inger, John, Joan;
front: Reggie, Erna, John, Suzanne, Anne.*

Material Changes in the Decorating Business

My painting and decorating work with John took us off to all kinds of places, including the Poldhu Hotel, Trelowarren, the Housel Bay Hotel at the Lizard and the old coastguard houses (through Government contracts at Cadgwith), Mullion, Porthleven and St Just. We were using a form of distemper in those days called Walpamur as plastic emulsion paints had not then come into use. Our first job using emulsion was at St Michael's Church in the early 1960s during Revd Moon's time there as the vicar.

For any outside painting on blockwork in the mid 1950s, we used a product called Snowcem. It was horrible stuff to use and we had to mix it as a powder with water. It dried too hard and tended to crack and give all sorts of problems. We were decorating the interior of a house on the Lizard and another firm was applying snowcem to the outside. Every night the men washed out their buckets and poured the remains down the drain. One Friday, the people living in the house were away and the Snowcem set hard, blocking the drains. We had torrential rain and the downstairs was all flooded out. Lessons were learnt from that experience.

In the very early days we used lime which had the great advantage of being breathable. We also made our own ceilingite, using Queensgate Whiting, and ordinary powder size. We used to boil up the glue size according to the instructions, put the Queensgate whiting to soak in a bucket over night and then make up the glue size with boiling water to pour onto the whiting. After several hours it would turn to a jelly, which we diluted down according to the state of the ceiling. Before the days of Polyfilla, cracks were filled with Alabastine. When Polyfilla came along it was marketed at half the price of Alabastine to capture and secure the market and then the price gradually went up and up. For fixing screws, etc., there was no such thing as rawplugs, so for outside work we used lead, and inside shaped wood, cutting the holes out with a hammer and chisel.

For wall-papering before the age of cellulose pastes, we made our own using flour and water. Mother had a large, black cast-iron kettle which would hold about six pints and we used to measure out the flour, add a little soda, pour in a drop of boiling water and stir to make a creamy constituency before pouring in the rest of the boiling water, stirring all the time. As long as the water was boiling the mixture would then go thick and, after being left over night, could be watered down ready for use. You can't beat flour and water paste, but it certainly takes time to make.

Every job I did gave me a great sense of satisfaction and that is what made the work so enjoyable. With painting and decorating, one could always see what one had done and if the customer was satisfied then so was I. I never got involved in colour schemes, I left this to the customer and I did not offer advice.

We did a lot of work for banks (*below*) mainly during the evenings and at weekends. We also worked a great deal for one Falmouth family; we decorated the house of the parents and also those of their sons and after that were asked whether we would be able to go to London to decorate their family flat there. When John told me that we had been invited I pictured the place as a reasonably sized bedsit. Instead of that it was a mansion, with art room, music room and five or six bedrooms. The lounge was huge. We used to go up by car and buy all our materials up there. There were five men and I did all of the cooking so my evenings were mostly spent buying the necessary food.

The same family also asked whether I knew of anyone who might be able to come and live with them and look after the children for a while. Inger suggested that Rancy, her cousin in Iceland, might like to come for a period to stay in England and this she did, travelling across and staying with the family for nearly 12 months. It was a wonderful opportunity for her and she had a marvellous time, with the family taking her everywhere they went.

Barclays Bank where John and Reggie did a great deal of decorating.

Kerrier Rural District Council and staff, mid 1930s. This photograph was taken outside The Willows.

*Helston Grammar School Football Team, 1947.
Left to right, back: Peter Rundle, Gerald Sobey, Stuart Mundy, Michael Rickard, Leonard Thomas, David Watts, David Emmett, Mr R.J. Holden;
front: Royston Howitt, Gerald Richards, Mr H.E. Dransfield, Frank Caddy, William Bromley.*

Helston – An Expanding Town

I had left Helston as a small but thriving town and when I returned there was little that seemed immediately to have changed. A closer look, however, showed what alterations war had brought; a new airfield was being created, new housing was required and the 1944 Education Act had been passed, bringing with it inevitable changes in the school system. A new Welfare State was also about to be created.

By August 1944 roads and footpaths within the area that became RNAS Culdrose had been closed under the Defence Regulations and a new main road was opened to traffic. Three farms – Content, Eglosderry and Killianker – were requisitioned and demolished. Our favourite walk had gone, as had the cricket pitch, the pavilion, and the cycle track.

Plans had been made to develop housing mostly on level ground between Clodgey Lane and Meneage Road. Five pre-fabricated bungalows were erected in Sanctuary Lane and named Beacon Crescent. Meanwhile, permanent housing was progressing at Beacon Parc. In August 1947 I was allocated No. 1 Trevenen Road and in May 1948, Trengrouse Way Car Park was opened. By 1950 new developments were being named Kingsley Way and Vyvyan Place and such was the pace of change that by November 1951 the 100th new council house was being allocated. The new shop and flats in Trengrouse Way opened in 1952 and around 1960 I lost part of my garden for road widening. The new fire station next door opened in July 1954.

Major reforms stemming from the 1944 Education Act affected the whole spectrum of school education in Helston with secondary education being made available to all children aged 11 or over. An infant school was established in the former Church Street Boy's School and the mixed Junior School was housed in the former National School which is now Andrew's Hall.

When my daughter Suzanne started school, she went to the small Infants School on the east side of Church Street which is now the practice room for the Helston Town Band. At the age of seven she transferred across the road to the mixed junior school. Mr Truscott was headmaster. That closed when she was 10 and she went then to St Michael's new building just off Trengrouse Way. This was in September 1957, the final year in Junior School. From here, in 1958, she went to Penrose Road School, which at the time locals called 'The Green School' because of the uniform. All the children from the Lizard area attended this establishment which was headed by a Mr Harris.

The back of Gilbert's shop which was sold in the early 1960s. Note the Horse & Jockey path sign and the entrance to the sports shop in the house at the rear of the court.

Pupil numbers increased rapidly with the expansion of the town and the new Secondary Modern School had to be built at Gwealhellis for pupils living in Helston and the immediate surrounding area. The children from the Lizard area continued to use the Penrose Road site, right up until Mullion School was built, but as a Helston child Suzanne had the good fortune to move into a brand new building in 1959. At that stage Mr Harris went to work as the head of a school in Camborne. Contemporaries of Suzanne at the 'Green School' included Joan, Rita and Sylvia Williams, whose parents farmed Landrivick at Manaccan. When their father died, their mother, Ruth, moved into Helston and started Ruth's Café in Meneage Street.

In the early 1950s our family did not have a car but we managed quite well without. Public transport was reasonably good and I generally cycled to and from work whilst Inger and Suzanne walked everywhere. At this time Trevenen Road only went down as far as the unit houses and there were fields beyond this where children could play in the trees. Council houses arrived in about 1956/57 and the houses across Trengrouse Way were built in the early 1970s.

The growing use of cars and buses lead to the closure of the railway station, a sad loss for the town. In 1964 the station, previously such a busy place, was demolished. Everything that came or went to Culdrose via the railway was never accredited to Helston Station as it was all paid for by the department in London. This Culdrose traffic was therefore ignored in the traffic audit which decided the station's fate and, had this been otherwise, one wonders whether the town might have kept its precious facility. Naturally when the railway closed down, so did the slaughtering businesses who all moved to Redruth.

During the post-war era, our family attended Church Street Chapel, and Suzanne and John went to the Sunday School there. This closed after Suzanne left the area at 18 and when she came back again to Helston ten years later, by then with her own children, they all went down to Sunday School at the Wesley Chapel in Coinagehall Street.

Helston County, Later Helston Grammar School

After the Education Act of 1944 Helston County School became a grammar school whilst Helston Secondary Modern School was formed in the Penrose Road buildings.

Above: *The new Helston County Secondary School building, opened on 6 February 1939.*

below: *Helston County School prospectus, c.1910.*

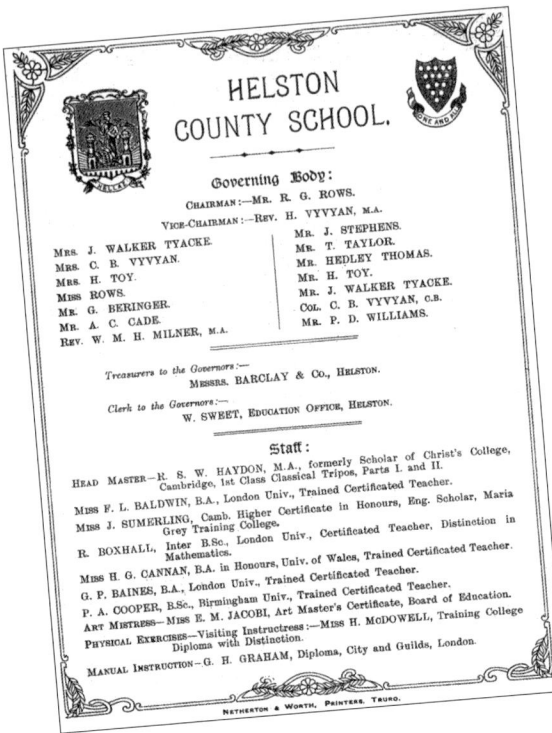

Top: *Senior pupils at the Grammar School, 1946. Left to right, back: David Stevens, Courtney Rowe, Stuart Mundy, Gerald Williams, Rex Carkeek, David Emmett; middle: Margaret Wood, Thelma Crowle, Sheila Clarke, Olive Hall, Susanne Eva; front: Francis Caddy, Mrs E.M. Sansom, Mr H.E. Dransfield, Mr L. Blewett, Rosemary Cowls.*

Above: *Helston Grammar School Staff, 1950. Left to right: ? Quick, L. Blewett, R.J. Holden.*

Chapter 7: Flora Day

No discussion of Helston would be complete without some mention of Flora Day. As a Helstonian, 8 May has always had a special significance for me. It is usually held on this date unless it falls on a Sunday or Monday, in which case it is held on the previous Saturday.

The origins of the Furry Dance, recorded in about 1700 by Daniel Defoe as 'an ancient and curious custom', are no longer known. After a shaky spell in the mid-Victorian period when it was in danger of abolition as an uncouth pagan ritual, the dance seems to have won the support of the local upper class, among them Squire Henry Rogers of Penrose, with the visit of the Lord Mayor Treloar in 1907 really putting Flora Day on the map. The linking of 'Flora' with the dance seems to have originated in a bogus, 18th-century attempt to establish a classical connection for it. The name has stuck to the festivities but it is now accepted that 'Furry' is the correct name for the dance. Certainly a pre-Christian ritual, it is essentially a spring festival expressing joy at the triumph of spring over winter. This date is also the feast of the Apparition of St Michael, Helston's, and Cornwall's, patron saint who it is said appeared over St Michael's Mount at Marazion in AD495. The saint is supposed to have spread his wings over Helston and was the slayer of the fiery dragon, the beast of darkness, hence representing the triumph of good over evil. For hundreds of years the dance, which has now become christianised, has been performed in the ancient town.

'Furry Day fever' starts in Helston soon after May Day and 7 May is spent decorating the houses and shops with greenery, bluebells and furze gathered from the surrounding countryside. The air of excitement can be felt by everyone. The children also take great delight in gathering the flowers and many hours are spent decorating the Guildhall.

At 6.30a.m. the bells of St Michael's Church hail the beginning of the day. The dances which involve the whole town, four in all, begin at 7.00a.m. with the last dance commencing at 5.00p.m. The children's dance was introduced in 1922 and I was dancing two years later, but had to wait until 1951 before I joined in the main midday dance. The first dance leaves from the Guildhall and was originally the servants' dance, staged at an early point in the day so that they could return to their duties. All dances are headed by the town's band followed by the Mayor of Helston and the dance stewards.

At 8.30a.m. the Hal-An-Tow arrives, a very noisy band of people bedecked with branches of sycamore, or 'Faddy' as it is known locally. The main spectacle of the Hal-an-Tow is the slaying of the dragon by St George. St Michael is then introduced with a song and slays the Devil, thus releasing the town's inhabitants from evil. The chorus rejoices with the words 'A Summer is a come O, and winter is a Gone O' and the ritual is thought to be the sole survivor of the original festivities. Just before 10a.m. the town centre fills rapidly with people of all ages, each eagerly awaiting the start of the children's dance which has become one of the most charming and delightful features of the day. More than 1000 children take part, all dressed in white. The girls of each school wear distinctive garlands in their hair and the boys wear their school ties with sprays of freshly-picked lily-of-the-valley pinned to their shirts. The teachers also have a very busy day escorting the children around the town in this, the largest procession of the day, and as the children wind their way up Coinagehall Street to the finish of the dance there is many a tired pair of feet.

Between the dances various groups perform in the streets – a great attraction for the children. With the approach of the midday dance the area around the Guildhall is packed with a seething throng and throughout the route, about two miles in length, thousands of people are content to stand awaiting the colourful spactacle. The dancers enter some of the shops and houses by one door, emerging from another, a ritual which is probably a survival of a purification rite or an act of driving out the spirit of darkness and bringing in that of light. Whatever its meaning Helstonians welcome the dancers and the happy spirit they bring with them into their homes. At Lismore the dancers take refreshments and a short, well-earned rest.

The leading two couples of all the dances must, according to tradition, be Helston born. The ladies spend many weeks preparing, some having their outfits specially made. For the principal dance at midday the gentlemen wear top hats and morning suits. The last dance at 5p.m. is a repeat of the early-morning dance, with the same dancers taking part. Helston Town Band, with help from musicians from other bands, always do the town proud and throughout the day will have walked about ten miles. The dance finishes at the Guildhall and, in the case of the midday dance, to the tune of the National Anthem.

Flora Day

Left: *Flora Day, c.1900. Here the dancers are shown on the bowling green, the men in their morning suits and bowler hats.*

Below: *Flora Day, 1946, the year when Mr A.H. Hawke's son led the midday dance.*

Below right: *Midday dance, 1923. Included are: Hedley Thomas and Miss K. Toy, E. Cunnack and Miss Phyllis Wakeham, J.M. Trezise and Miss Winnifred Courtis, Cpt Moreing MP and Miss May Hall, E. Courtis and Miss Alma Hendy, H.N. Vick and Miss Hood, Fred Cunnack and Miss Gwen Thomas, P.Q. Treloar and E. Thomas, Leslie Connack and Miss Marjorie Thomas, L. Treloar and Miss Hadley, E.H. Dunstan and Miss K. Rowe, R. Eathorne and Miss Irene Eathorne, Revd and Mrs Kempthorne.*

Below: *Children's Dance, 1951. Left to right: Garry Addison, David Hawke and Jasmine Coldrick, David Herriott and Jane Truscott, Jean Hill (who is dancing with her brother Anthony).*

Flora Day, 1951. Left to right: Joan, John, Inger and Reg Jenkin.

FLORA DAY

Clockwise from top: *Flora Day, 1953; Suzanne and John Jenkin (second couple from front) dancing in Lismore Gardens, 1978; Flora Day children's dance, 1947; Flora Day, 1927; Suzanne (second from left) with friends in 1956.*

Filming Flora Day at the early-morning dance in Meneage Street, early 1950s.

Dancing as a Pupil of the Wesley Day School (1924–1930)

The last time that I danced the Flora as a boy was in 1930. The children's dance was started at 10.30a.m. by 346 pupils drawn from Helston Church of England Day School, whose turn it was to lead the procession. Some 42 couples came from my school, and our accompanying teachers were Mr Hart the headmaster, Miss Winn, Miss Eddy and Mrs Oliver. Miss Cossentine's school was also represented and 75 couples came from the County School. The girls were dressed in white frocks bedecked with wreaths of flowers around their heads and we boys wore spic-and-span summer suits with button holes. Led by the town's band we danced through the streets to the Furry tune, making calls at the residences of Dr J.P. Michael, Mr Henry Toy (The Willows), Mr George Cunnack (Lismore) and Mr A.P. Ratcliffe (Penhellis), thence to the bowling green and back to the Corn Exchange for dismissal. At the end the Mayor of Helston (Alderman W.J. Trezise) said that times had changed a great deal since his own childhood when children were taken away from Helston on Flora Day and not permitted to participate in the proceedings. The change was all to the good and he hoped the children would grow up full of enthusiasm for the preservation of the historic celebrations.

In 1930 the Hal-an-tow was revived and 38 boys accompanied by members of Helston Old Cornwall Society (Revd G.H. Doble, Messrs T.J. Hart, J. Whitford, B.T. Rawlings, P. Cowls, F.P. Sandry, J.P. Rogers, H. Adams, A.S. Oates, G.H. Anthony, F.R. Trounson, W. Stephens) performed the bringing in of 'the summer and the May O' – represented by green boughs brought from St Johns. The company sang the ancient Hal-an-tow song, the accompaniment being supplied by Mr Lionel Wearne (violin), Mr Peter Williams (drum) and Mr Harry Thomas (triangle).

Suzanne Jenkin Recalls Flora Day

Preparation for Flora Day starts the year before, with the ladies spying out the dresses of the dancers in that year. In January one sends in one's application to the Secretary of the Flora Day Committee and then we start with the pattern book, looking at materials and waiting until we get an invitation. Some ladies go ahead and get their dresses made in anticipation of receiving an inivitation, only to be disappointed when it doesn't turn up! I have always waited until it arrives before starting, but will have a clear idea of what I am going to make.

When the invitation comes at the end of March or beginning of April there is a real air of excitement and the sewing machine and needles rattle away. Today there are not very many lady dancers who make their own dresses. A dress normally costs about £70 for the material and £40 to £50 for the work and there are many dress makers in and around Helston, Ebony, up on the Water-ma-Trout industrial estate, being one of the largest. Each has to be different as, once made, a dress will be used for one Flora Day only. Invitations are rare so everybody makes every effort to be original – it is an honour to dance on Flora Day, therefore one wants to look one's very best. We still have one or two boxes around the house containing past dresses. Most of the men hire their outfits – as did my brother John. This costs a further £55 and then of course there is always something to put in the steward's hat at the end of the dance – it is an expensive, but splendid occasion.

John and I usually danced together and always applied as a pair. Since my own children have been dancing they also do so together. In the years that John was away the invitation still came to both of us, but John could not always get home so for some years I had to find a partner.

One has to be 16 to apply to dance the early-morning dance and for those who are of a Helston family but not born in the town – such as Richard, John's eldest – the chances of being accepted are uncertain. The first dance of the day is a lovely event and the atmosphere in the town is fantastic, with a tremendous air of expectancy, the church bells ringing out in the background and a wonderful scent of the bluebells and lily of the valley.

I started taking part in Flora Day at school when I was seven and as a child it was my greatest ambition to dance. I well remember watching my mother and father dance in 1953. Every year I used ask when my turn would come. 'When you go to school, you can dance!' was the reply. I started school at five, Flora Day was coming up and all of the children were practising, but I had to wait another two years. It was made all the worse because I had a friend who lived up the road whose birthday fell before 8 May and who was able to dance one year before me. I still remember the disappointment.

Reg's granddaughter, Melanie Mahon, dancing with Robert Hall, 1986.

I danced for nine consecutive years at school, finishing in 1963. Our dresses often did more than one year, but of course we would wear them to parties, Sunday School anniversaries and all sorts of other dressed-up occasions. Some children when they left school danced in the early-morning dance and some stuck with it until they were 50! At primary school John danced with a little girl and it poured with rain all the way round. They were absolutely drenched, his partner cried every step of the way and John never wanted to dance again. He only returned to it at the age of 15 or 16 at the Secondary School.

I first danced in the midday dance in 1972 and have taken part in this particular event 11 times, the latest being 1997 when I stepped in for my daughter Melanie who was ill. I haven't had an invitation in my own right for several years and my own generation has stepped down now, in many instances leaving their children to take over.

Helston children come to school with a full knowledge of the steps, but others who have moved into the town find it suprisingly difficult to learn even the basics. Last year there were well over 1000 children dancing and it may be that the Helston Upper School will be incorporated into the early-morning dance.

Flora Day is still very much a family occasion. When John and Karen and I were in London we all came home for Flora Day and on occasions we have been as many as 13 overnight in the house, with beds and sleeping bags everywhere. We still get the same thrill when our children dance as we did ourselves a number of years ago.

One year when we didn't come back for the day Father rang me at seven in the morning and said 'I thought you would like to hear the Town Clock and the Band!!' John had come down to spend the day with us, so he was there to listen as well. Father continued with his phone calls at the start of every dance during the day and John and I made up our minds there and then that we wouldn't miss another Flora Day. I am looking forward to my granddaughter dancing in 2005 so that the family tradition will continue!

Helston's Bands

*A very early and faded photograph of a Helston band, c.1900.
Second from the left in the back row is Richard Laity of St Martin.*

*Helston Town Band, c.1928.
Left to right. back: C. Coombes, ?, Percy Bowden, ?, Charlie Wearne, V. Weare, Jim Busby,
Oates Williams;
centre: Dick Pascow, ?, Ted Uren, Jim Sharp, ?, ?, Ken Pascoe, Walter Wearne
front, sitting: Jack Pascoe, Harold Nichollas, Len Hender, Bert Busby, ?, ?, Harry Pascoe,
Dale Penaluna.*

Helston's Bands

This is thought to be a photograph of Helston Town Band at Plymouth in 1941.

Helston Town Band, 1953.
The photograph includes: Leslie Angove, ?, Ken Johns, Jim Busby, Reg Busby, Denis Chritophers, Verny Wear, Ernie Reynolds, Gordon Chanter, Ted Uren, Jack Tucker, ?, Ed Ashton, Alwyn Williams, Jim Sharp, Russel Harvey, Colin Hocking, Bert English, J. Medlyn, Edwin Lane, ? Wilcocks, Clifford Thomas, Roy Uren, John Harvey, Harry Pascoe, Walter Wearne, A. Watts, Fred Pascoe, Dale Penaluna, Will Wear, Ken Pascoe, Mrs Hender, Ken Hinks, Ed Cunnack, Len Hender, Mr Eade, Mrs Alwyn Williams.

Helston Town Band at Bude, 1941.

Chapter 8: Reggie in Retirement 1980–2000

MISSING SISTERS & THE SYMONS FAMILY

It was my sister Erna who started me off in the hunt for my family when she gave me the Bible which my father used during his time in the Navy. Inside the cover was a list of all the names and birth dates of his brothers and sisters. I had always thought that he had been born in Camborne but, after finding no trace at the town's Registry Office, I went to Redruth to get a copy of his birth certificate. I then did some work on the censuses and gradually gathered information together.

When researching old issues of the *West Briton* in 1986 I chanced upon a piece about my father's first wife's funeral, in which 'Revd H. Hewitson expressed his sympathies for Mr Henry Jenkin and his three children'. News that my father had been married before came as something of a shock. The lady was called Symons and they had three daughters – my half sisters, Erne, Lily and Mary. I then started hunting the *West Briton* in search of any mention of them and came across reports of concerts at the Epworth Hall where they had recited poems and sung. Reports continued from time to time until 1909 when all clues stopped. From this point on I searched without success.

I remembered that Father used to get a letter from South Africa which Mother would put on the mantlepiece for him. This he would take into the sitting room to read and nothing was ever said about it. In Redruth Library I read *Cornish Emigrants to South Africa* and discovered that a Humphrey Symons from Meneage Street had gone to Kimberley, South Africa. Was this a possible link? In fact, he turned out to be the girls' uncle and I wondered whether they had gone out to live with him. Having obtained a copy of his will, I was able to establish that the girls were not beneficiaries, from I was able to get the name of his family. I then wrote to a Mr Lambert Truran (then a member of the Cornwall Family History Society) who suggested that I write to all those with the surname Symons in South Africa. I sent off hundreds of letters but received not a single reply. By now, however, I was fairly certain that my three half-sisters had gone to South Africa, where I put out an appeal on radio; to my great delight I had a positive response and as a result have learnt a great deal more about the three girls and their familes.

After their mother's death from cancer in 1907 (see page 28) the three girls continued to live in Helston with Grandmother Elizabeth Symons at 77 Meneage Street, but she too died, on 4 October 1909. The girls then moved to St Austell to the home of their Aunt Bessie Sweet, a widow, whose husband had died from 'miner's chest' and the three sisters shared a house with four other children. In 1912 Humphrey Symons' sister, Nellie Trennick, returned from South Africa and took Erna back with her to live with Humphrey in Kimberley. In 1913, Nellie returned to England with her four children and took a house in Dawlish. Mary came to help with the children and Nellie paid for her to have lessons in shorthand and typing. Lily and Mary stayed in St Austell until 1919 when they too went out to live with Uncle Humphrey in South Africa.

Erna married Barklett Fitzgerald Guiney at Queenstown, South Africa. The chief smelter in Benoni, he died on 30 March 1960 in Johannesburg. Erna lived in a lovely little coastal village in the cape known as Fishoek and was by all accounts a very dignified person, a lover of good literature, mentally very active, and ran the Library Book Club at the Modder East Mine where her husband worked. Bob was a fine man, kind and considerate and although he had lost a leg due to infection after an accident (before the days of antibiotics), he went on working under difficult conditions in the smelting works on the mine. Like many mothers Erna pinned her ambition on her son, Norman, who had a university education, only to lose him as a trainee pilot during the war.

Lily (Betty) Jenkin married Harold Bradshaw who was a purser on board the ship on which she journeyed out to South Africa. Betty trained as a nurse at Johannesburg General Hospital, became a Sister and later married. She was a very practical, common-sense person, and, together with her husband, enjoyed a good lifestyle.

Mary Jenkin was known as Marian and, having taken her shorthand lessons, worked in a bank and married the manager. Mary suffered with terrible migraines which meant that Kay Field, who lived with the family, actually did most of the running of the house. Mary's husband, John Jeans, died in 1955, by which time their daughters Shirley and Pamela were both married to Naval officers at Simon's Town.

Beating the bounds, 1928, with Mayor John Bennett Martin.

Beating the bounds, 1934. Mayor Alderman, W.J. Rogers, leads the beaters.

Exploring The Past

During my retirement I have had great fun exploring old Helston with old friends like Bill Scott, Bill Rogers and Martin Matthews. We meet on Saturdays at the Helston Folk Museum, talking, swapping memories, turning up photographs and finding out as much as possible about Helston. Martin has been much involved in the re-designing and extension of the Folk Museum which should remain a wonderful asset to the town. Admission is still free for local ratepayers. Bill Scott and I have been much involved in the development of the Town Trail and Bill Rogers and I have come together to help with ancient ritual of 'Beating the Bounds'.

Beating the Bounds

The ancient borough of Helston, granted a charter by King John in 1201, is widely believed to have been marked out using a stone at three corners and a tuft of grass at the fourth. The actual boundary followed an irregular perimeter enclosing lands and houses owned by burgesses. The boundaries of the parishes were established in a similar way and in the days before maps it was essential to walk them regularly to guard against encroachments. Local boys were taken on the route and bumped against trees, walls or posts, so that when they grew up some would be able to pass on their knowledge of the boundary to the next generation. This ancient ritual of 'beating the bounds' is one that has been in existence in Helston since the second charter of Queen Elizabeth in 1585.

Before 1934, the Borough of Helston encompassed a relatively small area and only three stones remain in position on the inner boundary. They can be found on the Redruth road, Church Hill and at Prospect Place. In 1934 the boundaries were extended to include Porthleven and parts of the parishes of Sithney and Wendron – forming the modern Borough of Helston. In 1985 the boundaries were changed again, when Helston and Porthleven separated to become independent parishes. The boundaries of the new Helston Town Parish were at the same time extended towards Trenethick, Lowertown, Sithney and Porthleven. One third of the boundaries are beaten each year and in 1999 the Mayor of Helston and members of the Town Council, together with local schoolchildren, traced the north-west boundary from the Lowertown junction on the Redruth road to Penventon Farm.

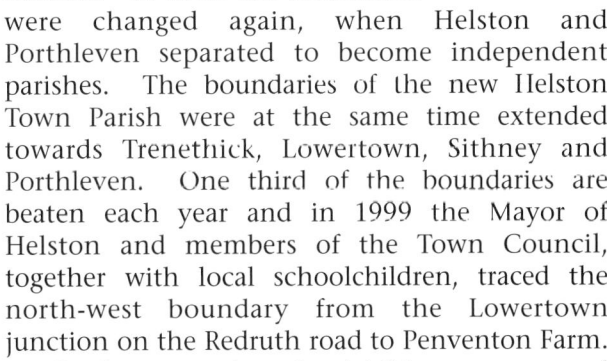

In days gone by schoolchildren were armed with sticks for the ritual. A sod of turf was cut, which was then beaten with sticks, a sprig of May was stuck into the turf and three cheers were given. Some of the children were then turned upside down to have their heads bumped on the turfed stone.

The beating of the bounds still continues in a number of places in the country. It seems to have been connected with, or to have derived from, the ancient Rogationtide processions, when it was customary for the parish priest, along with the choir and servers, to go through the fields near the Parish church singing Litanies and asking for God's blessing on the crops. This accounts for the fact that the beating of the bounds at Helston normally takes place on the eve of Ascension Day.

Beating the bounds, 1999. Derek Wolf, Town Clerk, is about to bounce Reg Jenkin with the help of Clinton Endean, on the boundary stone at Squire's Lane. Graham Williams, Mayor, is lending vocal support.

Helston Valley Tin Company

Our historical group have had a great time finding out about this company, both through written sources and through investigating the site itself. In his book *Wendron Tin Streamers* Justine Brooke, Bard 'Whythrer Stenoryon' – Researcher of Tinners, had this to say about the Helston Valley Tin Company:

Modern methods arrived in the summer of 1912, when boring operations were carried out between Helston and Loe Pool by a well-known company not mentioned by name. It probably used Banka drills which had been introduced to Cornwall two years earlier. To work the deposits the Merton Metallurgical Co. Ltd. of London formed a subsidiary called the Helston Valley Tin Co. Ltd., registered at the end of the year and the first limited company to work a tin-stream in the district. The Cornwall correspondent of the Mining Journal *reported in February 1913 that he had been informed that bore-holes put down to discover the depth of Payable dirt, before reaching the bedrock, had passed through an average depth of 25 feet of silt, which had evidently come from the Wendron and neighbouring mines. It lay on about seven feet of sea sand, which in turn lay on 20 to 30 feet of peat. Directly between the peat and the bedrock lay from 4 to 8 feet of alluvial rich in tin. The writer was assured the alluvial contained twice as much tin as the silt, although only the latter would be worked, and gave values which would make handsome profits for the proprietors. Although the sand and peat should have, perhaps, been measured in inches rather than feet, the presence of sea-sand indicates that the trials were made not far upstream from the head of Loe Pool.*

In June 1913 the Helston Valley Company obtained a 31 year lease from the Duchy at 1-20th dues, and under the management first of Richard Hall and then of M.S. Stuchbury proceeded to lay out a dressing plant at Castle-Wary some 80 feet above the water level of the recently constructed ornamental lake at Helston and about half a mile from the town.

The tin-bearing silt was first pumped into concrete storage tanks which delivered it by gravity to concave round frames, called Wilfley tables and Borlase buddles, with the coarser residues being pumped separately for future treatment if necessary. The whole was driven by two steam engines, one of which drove a 69 amp, 220 volt dynamo. Later in 1913 Edward Gammon was appointed assayer, and a Mr Vine of Camborne, former manager of the Bracket Tin Stream at Brea, was called to assist the manager.

The team brought the plant into production just before the outbreak of the First World War. The plant was closed down within about twelve months of starting. In October 1919 practically the whole of the company's capital was offered for sale by the Merton company, then in liquidation, and in August 1920 the machinery and materials were put up for sale. Prospecting at the Loe Pool in 1929 did not lead to any working, but concrete tanks, foundations, walls and a buddle built by the Helston Valley company, now much overgrown, can still be seen on the hillside above the road to lower Nansloe, a short distance south of the sewage-works.

Helston Valley Tin Company. Left to right: ?, Dick Laing, ?, ? Jory, Nat Wear, Dick Tremelling, ?, Fred James. The men are pictured dressing a plant at Castle Wary, Helston.

John Rapson, Champion Coal Carrier, 1953.

John Rapson
Champion Coal Carrier

Our history group's picture shows Johnny Rapson, the coal-carrying delivery man entering the Seven Star's Pub, now the Fitzsimmons Arms. His was a familiar face around Helston delivering coal for Harvey & Co whose depot was near Helston Railway Station. In 1953 he decided that he would contest the feats of coal-carrying performed by Mr Wild of Wiltshire and Mr Miners from Tregony. At that time the actual records were:

three-and-a-half miles in 1 hour and 20 minutes set by Mr Wild
four miles in 59½ minutes, set by Mr Miners

On 14 February 1953, his 33rd birthday, Johnny Rapson set a new record by walking 5½ miles in 1½ hours. The very next day Mr Wild did 6½ miles in 2¼ hours. Not to be outdone, Johnny, on 21 February, carried a 100-cwt bag of coal the same distance in 1 hour, 54 minutes and 50 seconds. On 28 February he did 7¼ miles from Camborne Town Clock to Sithney School in 1 hour, 46 minutes and 15 seconds.

Since that time no other challenger has beaten the record, although Mr Wild did set up a new record of 13 miles in 5 hours, 5 minutes and 30 seconds, with three stops on the way.

On 4 April Johnny carried 100 cwt of coal the 14 miles from Perranporth to Camborne in 3 hours and 40 minutes non-stop. After this extraordinary feat in 1953 Johnny earned himself an entry in the *Guiness Book of Records* as 'Champion Coal Carrier'.

He did all of his carrying with ordinary household coal in regulation coal sacks. He did not use any pads and wore ordinary clothes and boots. He trained in his garden for four to five hours twice weekly, his main hobby was roller skating and from time to time he would do this with a 100-cwt sack of coal on his back! He had no special diet apart from drinking the odd glass of milk.

On 27 May 1983, Bryan Newton increased the non-stop, long-distance coal-carrying record to 32 miles in 10 hours and 18 minutes from Leicester to the Nottingham border.

Old Time Dance Club of Helston, 1950.

Trenear Dairy, c.1932.
Left to right, back: B. Pooley, Will Carlyon, J. Jeffery, Jack Williams, Laurie Goldsworthy, Phill Trezise, Sydney Gregg, Hartley Drew, Cyril Treloar, Tom Eddy; front: ? Bosustow, Nora Bosustow, Vera Jewell, Doris Winn, Doreen Pellow, Ernest Richards. Note the two small lorries in the background.

Conclusion

In the middle of the Nineteenth Century, my Grandfather Benjamin left Cornwall and took his wife and five children around Cape Horn in a sailing vessel to Bolivia in order to carry on his job as a miner. The whole family returned six years later to the Borough of Helston, which was then a thriving leather town. I still marvel at the confidence of these Victorian Cornish people, to set off and travel such great distances. In their early twenties, his three eldest sons returned to Bolivia and Chile to continue with a mining career, one returned to Cornwall in middle age, the other two remained. John married locally, becoming a Catholic and changing his name to Juan, and became fully integrated into the local population. My father, grandfather's youngest son, having served his time as an engineer, ran away to sea, to avoid becoming a miner. He saw the growth of the great Imperial British Navy, sailing the seas around the world and retiring in 1907 as a Chief Petty Officer after 21 years service. I, as his third son, little expected to travel anywhere, but the advent of the internal combustion engine and a Second World War was to change all that.

As a family growing up, we used to walk everywhere, apart from the occasional trip in a pony and jingle and the annual chapel rail trip from Helston Station to Carbis Bay. My first ride in a motorised vehicle was in the charabanc for the chapel trip to Kennack Sands – I was most impressed on the way out, but unfortunately the engine broke down on the way back, and of course in those days there were no such things as public telephones, no other motorised traffic, so we had no other choice but to walk all the way back. Soon, however, motorised buses became a common form of transport. How was I to know that I too would travel the world in my retirement, thanks to gaining my attractive Norwegian wife who encouraged me to remain active, and a son who worked throughout the world.

I look back over the years and marvel at all of the changes – earth closets to flush toilets; hand-operated outside water pumps to indoor water at various taps throughout the house; candles and oil lamps to electric lights controlled at the switch of a button; our first cat's-whisker radio to modern radios. Televisions and VCRs; the telegraph network with its telegrams to internet with its e-mail; handwritten letters to telephone chats; galvanised baths to modern showers; Shank's pony to world jet flights; locally-grown food to food from across the world – and the man on the moon is no longer a figment of imagination.

Charabanc outing, c.1920s. The passengers include Mr and Mrs M. Willey, Mrs Bray, Mr Haynes, Leslie Willey, Harry Thomas, Clifford Bray.

A Developing Town

Left: *The building on the far left of the picture is Taylor's Tyre Centre which is due for replacement, and the Peugeot Show Room is planned to have an alternative use.*

Right: *Clodgey Lane roundabout leading to Tesco's. This was once a narrow country lane.*

Left: *Converting the Poor Law Institution into flats.*

Right: *The new Helston Garages building.*

CONCLUSION

The sounds also are so different – I rarely hear the 'moaning of the bar' or the dawn chorus – street lights which are on all night haven't helped with this; the Lizard Fog Horn when the wind was in the right direction and of course the whistle and puff of the engine at the railway station. Laying snuggly wrapped up in bed, one could listen to the trickling of the kennel waters, the fretting of the horses, the lowing of the cattle in the fields around the house, and first thing in the morning the rattle of the milk churns. During the daytime, we had the calling by the fish sellers and the clatter of hob-nail boots on the pavements. Of course, on Saturdays, we had all the hustle and bustle of late night shopping and the Salvation Army Band playing at various stations within the town, one of which was right outside our house. All I get now is the roar of jet aircraft, the throb of helicopters and the racing of car engines. We lost the one pound and the ten-shilling notes, the florin and the half crown and the present one-pound coin is treated as if it was a 'tanner' of my childhood. If that wasn't enough they now weigh me in kilograms instead of stones and a one pound pot of jam is 454 grams!

Several place names have gone – Cinder Path, Foundry Road, Mason's Row, Penventon Lane, but some of the new names are very appropriate, Trengrouse Way, Anson Way, Hitchens Road. Gone, too, are those allotments with their lovely fresh vegetables; there was nothing to beat young potatoes dug straight from the soil or the perfect pea from the plucked green pod and the freshly drawn carrot; I thought I would never admit it, but I even miss Dad's 'Herbie Beer'!

The characters are so different – how I miss John Henry Julian, the Town Crier, Miss Roscollar the Bill-poster, Mr Jeffery the coalman who used to bring the coal indoors and dump it in the 'spence', the cupboard under the stairs. Then of course we had the street singer – 'Cuckoo Holmes', whose imitation of the cuckoo made him quite well known.

Over the last century, we have had 46 different Mayors, including two ladies, the majority of whom worked very hard on behalf of the Borough, including four members of the Rogers family. The sizes of the congregations in the various churches have fallen drastically, and yet, since the war, three new churches have been built in the town. We must accept that our town is continually changing. For example, just one recent edition of the *West Briton* gave us the following details:

The old Flora Cinema and the Flora Centre Project is on course for a September 2000 completion. The original Baptist Chapel, later the Flora Cinema, in Wendron Street, will be converted into a new

Top: *Ex-Flora Cinema being converted into a new cinema and fitness gymnasium*
Above: *Fighter plane at Culdrose.*

80-seater air-conditioned cinema, a cardiovascular gymnasium suite, a cafe and four start-up business units.

Derelict cottages in The Clies have been refurbished to accommodate office premises and the 'Flying Start' Nursery, for pre-school children. The latter recently launched a new out-of-school fun club, on its upper floor, with places for 24 school-aged children.

On June 21 2000, 824 Squadron was commissioned as a training squadron for aircrew and engineers who will fly the Merlin helicopter in operational squadrons. It will provide integrated flying training and ground-based simulator instruction for all air crew, making extensive use of advanced computer based training facilities. 824 Squadron will receive 12 Merlin HM Mk1 helicopters and since Culdrose is the operating base for the Merlin helicopter which will serve in aircraft carriers and type 23 frigates and other warships. The skies around Helston will not be empty or silent for several years to come.

A procession through the town 21 July 1923.

CONCLUSION

Nos 1–3 Trevenen Road, a pair of Cornish units, built immediately after the Second World War. All have been refurbished, the external walls of the lower floor were removed completely and rebuilt, whilst the upper floor was suspended on jacks. Reg Jenkin occupies No. 1, and has lived there since it was first built.

Plans have been submitted to remove the Taylor's Tyres derelict site. This has been an eyesore at the top of Meneage for far too long. The plans include a single-storey office building facing Grange Road, with 60 parking spaces and landscaping – are we to have some trees planted in a Helston car park? Lismore Garden was a delight on Flora Day.

What a legacy those Victorians left for future generations – how do we measure up? Some things never change. In 1841 11 families from Helston, five of them from one street, sailed to New Zealand to find work and to start a new life. Two of the families came from the building community, the Georges and the Evas, others were miners. The Moyles were rope makers. All landed in Taranaki where they laid the roots for the new city of New Plymouth. Both the building families took a hand in building the Parish Church of St Mary's. In May 2000, Stephen Lay, a resident of Wendron, flew out to join other 'Cousin Jacks' in the search for gold in Georgia. This was very much like the pioneers of the past, the difference being that Stephen commutes from his home in Cornwall to an office in Georgia, whereas the pioneers did not return to this country, although many of their offspring have made journeys to the land of their forefathers. The time Stephen Lay takes to get from Wendron to London is about the same time as it takes him to get from London to his office in Georgia. Helston and the Lizard peninsula remain isolated as far as transport is concerned, but ironically communications to and from the area are as good as anywhere in the world.

We must ensure that the changes being made are for the betterment of this and future generations. Those who cannot remember the past are condemned to repeat it!

So, what of the future? Helston is no longer the hub of the surrounding countryside – out-of-town shopping and the motor car have contributed to its demise in this direction, as have the attraction of magnet towns like Truro and Exeter. Helston was once a great town with a tremendous tradition, but its sense of community, like many places elsewhere, appears to be disappearing. What caused this? Was it the over-reliance on Culdrose for providing jobs and its major boost to the economy? Did the closing of the railway station, 40 years ago, signal the death-knell to the town? How much has the Borough suffered as a result of its Council losing its real power to the District Council? Has education given sufficient attention to developing service to society? Have the planners had the best interests of Helston at heart? What is the plan for the next 50 years? If Culdrose closes what will happen – is there a contingency plan in place?

Helston expanded rapidly; there are about twice as many people here now as there were at the end of the Second World War. Initially the Borough appeared to adapt itself well to changing circumstances. It tried very hard to preserve its

145

Sir Edwin Durning Lawrence, a Cornish MP 1895–1906. A Liberal Unionist, Lawrence supported Mr Chamberlain's social program. This photograph was taken during the electioneering campaign of 1910 when he was defeated.

CONCLUSION

identity, and its independence within a wider context. There still exists a keen interest in local affairs; townspeople keep up the good traditions of the past, but major decisions, which affect us all, are now made well away from the town. Most of the great Helston families, who held the well-being of the town close to their hearts, have disappeared. It rests with the present Helston townspeople to stand for office and work for the good of their town. Helston has produced many worthy, successful and distinguished people in different walks of life – champions at sport, great inventors, magical musicians and passionate poets. Now that we are starting on the third millennium, Helston needs to take a good look at itself and plan for its future. Whatever happens, I feel confident that Helston as a town will rise to the challenge of regaining its ability to truly serve the population of the area, and Helstonians themselves will, as a result, continue to grow in stature. Might the town become one of international significance, with its own airport, a well preserved Victorian town centre with market stalls and traditional trades, similar to that of Williamsburg, in Virginia, USA, backed up by wonderful historical sites and centres of activities within the surrounding countryside; supplemented by a well-educated populace working in congenial high-tech industries, and living in a delightful part of the world where the best of nature is conserved, and the good traditions of the past are maintained.

Mr Andrew George, Liberal Democrat MP, 2000. The MP for St Ives constituency, he is pictured here beating his drum as part of the Hal-an-Tow on Flora Day, 6 May 2000.

*Left to right, back: A.H. Hawke, Lily Peters, Edgar Hawke;
front: Dorothy Hawke, Clara Hawke (née White), David Hawke, Emily Peters
(née White).*

Friends at No.5 Meneage Street, 1930s.

CONCLUSION

THE HAWKE FAMILY

When Alfred H. Hawke died in 1958, he left behind a fine collection of cards showing transport, adverts, dress and pastimes of his lifetime, some of which appear in this book. His photographs published in national newspapers did much to publicise Helston and its Flora Day.

Above: *Richard Hawke of Bristol, father of A.H. Hawke, Helston's famous photographer.*

Above right: *Eliza Hawke (née Burn), his wife.*

Right: *Mrs Clara Hawke and her mother Mrs White before the First World War.*

Below: *A photograph taken on 9 August 1911 of Clara with her daughter Dorothy, who died young.*

Below right: *A.H. Hawke (left) with fellow members of the Royal Flying Corps, 1918.*

Above: *Mrs Hawke with her sons, mid 1920s. A.H. Hawke was fond of his car and often used one on his many photographic postcards.*

Right: *The staircase at No. 5 Meneage Street.*

Helston Communications Workers

Clockwise from top: *Telegram boy, 1920s; Miss Ethel Hill, postlady, c.1916; Maud Richards, postlady, c.1916; Miss Roscollar, bill-poster, who worked with her brother Tom (Tomtweet), who was also the town crier; Mr Rowe, postman at Helston Station, c.1930.*

CONCLUSION

MAYORS AND REGALIA

In his book *The History of Helston* Spencer Toy set out a list of the town's mayors from 1714 through to 1935. Included in this volume is a similar list for the past 100 years, together with an account of some of Helston's regalia. For a period Helston and Porthleven formed a joint council and during that time the mayors were elected alternately from each town. In the list those with 'P' alongside their name came from Porthleven.

The official chain of office was purchased by private subscription in 1894 at a cost of £263. It is of 18-carat gold and is hallmarked throughout. It consists of a badge, a large centre link, a centre festoon link and a series of forty shields with ornamental connections. These shields form a considerable length and are festooned in two rows. On the obverse are elaborate monograms relating to the donors whilst on the reverse are inscriptions. The central festoon link is decorated with the royal arms, crest and motto treated in enamel and displayed against a large star. On the back is the name of the donor, 'Richard Skewes Martyn, J.P., Mayor 1881, 1890, 1891'. Below this is the central, oval-shaped link bearing the Cornish arms and motto, 'One and All', above which are the feathers and motto of the Prince of Wales. Inscribed also are the details of the donor:

Frederick Vivian Hill, J.P., C.C., Councillor 1868 to 1871, 1872 to 1877; Alderman 1877; Mayor 1872, 1874 to 1878, 1882, 1884 to 1886.

The badge is an elaborate piece of enamel work, its chief feature being a representation of the borough arms, with the maces beneath, and the inscription 'Insignia communitatis yule de Helleston-burgh'. This badge was 'Presented by James Rogers Pascoe of Pyrmont, Woodford, Essex, to the Corporation of his Native Town, 1894'.

Above: *William John Rogers, Mayor of Helston 1934–37.*
Below: *Helston Bowling Club, 1979 with Mayor Richard Lionel Rogers.*

THE BOOK OF HELSTON

Left: *Mr Hedley Thomas with the new fire engine, c.1909.*

Right: *William Thomas Rogers who was Mayor from 1974 to 1977.*

Left: *Mr Jack Rogers with Revd Moon on his left, 1953.*

Right: *Richard Lionel Rogers who was Mayor from 1978 to 1980.*

Mr and Mrs W.T. Rogers, 1974.

20th-Century Mayors of the Borough of Helston

1900–02	George Beringer
1902–03	Alfred Randle Thomas
1903–05	Richard Gundry Rapson
1905–07	Henry Toy
1907–08	Alfred Randle Thomas
1908–09	George Beringer
1909–10	Hedley Thomas
1910–12	Francis Henry Cunnack
1912–14	Henry Toy
1914–19	William Hall
1919–20	John Bennett Martin
1920–21	William James Johns
1921–24	Henry Toy
1924–26	William James Johns
1926–29	John Bennett Martin
1929–30	William John Trezise
1930–34	Henry Toy
1934–37	William John Rogers P
1937–40	Ernest Joseph Chappell
1940–42	Leonard Wilson Oliver P
1942–44	John Hedley Benney
1944–45	Edwin Upex
1945–46	Susan Bawden Coles P
1946–49	John Henry Adams
1949–51	William Reed Johns P
1951–53	John Rogers
1953–55	Joseph Alfred Strike Pascoe P
1955–57	Francis Joseph Moyle
1957–59	Francis Edynean Strike B.E.M. P
1959–61	James Henry Thomas
1961–62	Frederick Zieman P
1962–64	Arthur Evelyn Lee
1964–66	Michael George Gale P
1966–68	John Osborne Westcott Noye
1968–70	George Andrews P
1970–72	William Henry Scott
1972–74	Olive Lewis Holland P
1974–77	William Thomas Rogers
1977–78	Jeffery Roberts P
1978–80	Richard Lional Rogers
1980–81	Jeffery Roberts P
1981–83	Donald James Eddy
1983–84	Charles James Thomas
1984–85	David Priestley Balme P
1985–87	Franklyn Albert Moyle
1987–89	Donald James Eddy
1989–91	Ronald Williams
1991–93	John Hocking
1993–95	Brenda Anne Banfield
1995–97	Joseph Henry Michael Keay
1997–99	Graham Lester Williams
1999–	John Hocking

CONCLUSION

The forty shields bear the following inscriptions:

William Bolitho, Junr., High Sheriff of Cornwall 1895

William Bickford-Smith, M.P. for Truro-Helston Division 1885 to 1892

Hugh Rogers Mayor 1749 (presented by Capt. Rogers, R.A.).

Humphrey Millet Grylls, Mayor 1817, 1822, 1827, 1832

Glynn Grylls, Mayor 1836, 1838, 1841, 1844, 1850, 1853, 1854 (presented by his son, C.R. Gerveys Grylls)

Matthew Paul Moyle, Mayor 1849 (presented by his daughters, Constantia and Frances)

Thomas Hyne Edwards, Mayor 1855, 1856, 1866, 1868

Thomas Phillips Tyacke, Mayor 1857, 1861, 1862 (presented by his sons, Thomas and Joseph Sidney Tyacke)

James Clarke, Mayor 1863 to May 1864 (presented by his son, Sidney Clarke)

William Trevenen, J.P., Mayor May 1864, Nov. 1864, 1880, 1887 to 1889

Frederick Penberthy, J.P., Mayor 1867 (presented by his sister, Mrs. Lanyon, and her four daughters)

Richard Kirby, Mayor 1873, 1879 (presented by his son, Richard Kirby)

William Dale, J.P., Mayor 1883; Councillor 1876 to 1892; Alderman 1892

Albert Edward Ratcliffe, Mayor 1892, 1893; Councillor May, 1892

Charles Courtenay Hocking, J.P., Mayor 1896, 1897; Councillor 1896 to 1898; Alderman 1900

Alexander Pengilly, Mayor 1898, 1899; Councillor 1896.

George Beringer, J.P., Mayor 1900, 1901, 1908; Councillor 1891

Charles Lemon Frazer Daniell, J.P., Alderman 1877 to 1880; Councillor 1870 to 1873

James Woolcock, Alderman 1873 to 1879; Councillor 1854 to 1859 (presented by his daughter, Mrs. George Lanyon)

Thomas Taylor, Councillor March 1881

John Goldsworthy Reed, Councillor May 1892

Charles Frederick Dale, Councillor 1892

Edward Pownall Kendall, J.P., Councillor 1874 to 1892

William Woolcock, Councillor 1852 to 1859 (presented by his daughter, E. P. Woolcock)

William Chappell, Councillor 1874 to 1880 (presented by his widow)

William Sleeman, Councillor 1853 to 1856, 1860 to 1863 (presented by his son and daughters)

Odger Eva, Councillor 1881 to 1890; Borough Surveyor 1890

Joseph Walker Tyacke, Councillor 1877 to 1892; Town Clerk 1892

John James, Councillor 1892

John Oates Eva, Councillor April 1892

John Michael Martyn, Councillor 1887

William Penrose, J.P., Councillor 1865 to 1868, 1869 to 1892, 1893

Frederick Hill, Town Clerk 1834 to 1874 (presented by his son, H. Grylls Hill)

Richard Cotton, J.P., 1893

George James Cunnack (Connack), J.P., 1893

Charles Hosken, Borough Accountant, 1890 to 1892

Nicholas Trevenen Trengrouse, Borough Treasurer, 1857 to 1888 (presented by his sons, Henry and Richard Trengrouse)

John D. Wood, C.E., Helston

John Dale, Clerk of the Peace, 1869 to 1884 (presented by his sons, W. and C. F. Dale)

Walter Wearne, Medical Officer of Health, 1885

The remainder of the municipal insignia comprises two maces, two constable's poles, an armlet, a mayor's hat, and robes and hats for the sergeants-at-mace.

The maces (below) were presented to the borough by Lord Godolphin in 1777 and bear the inscription Godolphin. They are of silver gilt and are carried by means of ebony shafts of the baluster pattern, terminating in knobs of gold. The mace heads, attached by means of long, enriched, hollow joints or sockets, are adorned with scroll and foliaged work, and medallions containing representations of St Michael encountering the dragon, with a fortified town in the background. The heads are finished with circlets and a cresting of fleur-de-lis and crosses, from which spring the open arches of the crowns.

The constable's poles were presented by R.S. Martyn in 1882. The armlet is the oldest piece of the municipal insignia and is thought to have been presented by Robert Cock in 1676; it bears the inscription H.B., 1676, Robert Cock, Mayor. The mayoral hat was presented by the late George Beringer.

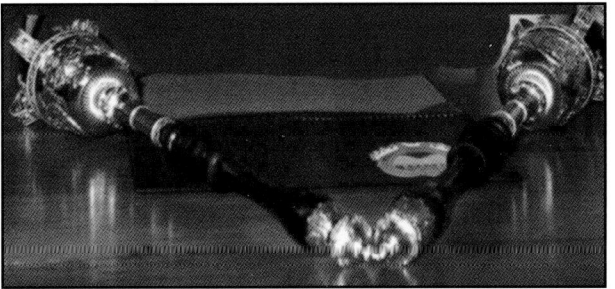

Helston Football Club, 1899.
Left to right, back: Mr Albert Rowe (trainer), Mr W.J. Oates, H. Pascoe, T. Banfield, A. Frazier, W.T. Rogers, Billy Williams, G. Lanyon;
centre: F. Dawe, ? Rose (with ball), Ted West;
front: W.J. Perring, J. Pearce.

Helston Cricket Club, 1970s.
Left to right, back: Les Reynolds, David Osborne, David Step, John Liddicoat, Ted Patel, John Richards, Lionel Step, Gus Hendy;
front: Tony Drew, Cyril Halloway, Reg Osborne, Robin Willoughby, Brian Gentry.

CONSLUSION

Helston Football Team, 1906/7. The picture includes ? Rodda (far left, back row), John Toy (second from left, back row), ? Charles (park keeper, far right, back row), ? Stephens (a baker, second from left, middle), Josiah Roberts (third from left, middle), John James (a postman, far right, middle).

*Helston Football Club, c.1936/7.
Left to right, back row: Jack Billing, ? Stephens, Reg Treloar, Harold Stallard, Nell Downing, Henry James, ?, A. Perry, Cyril Read, Perry Jenkin, Jack Rowe, Granvill Rogers, B.T. Rawlings, Jim Gilbert, Lionel Knowles;
front: A. Gilbert, Charlie Paynter, Rex Hart, Clifford Casley, R.O. Gilbert, W. Johns, ? Barnicoat.*

View of the church from an early 20th-century postcard.

The same scene in 2000.

Helston at the Start of the Twenty First Century

The first decade of the 21st Century has brought many changes to Helston and its immediate neighbourhood. Much new building has taken place both within the town itself and on new green field sites. The old Cattle Market has been given a new lease of life, the old Helston railway line is emerging from the bushes and the population is steadily increasing. RNAS Culdrose, which covers over 607 hectares, employs in excess of 3,000 service personnel, contractors and civil servants. It remains the largest single site employer in Cornwall and is one of Europe's largest helicopter bases. A new relief road has been built on the eastern side of town. The building of three new supermarkets has greatly affected the retail businesses in the centre of town, however it still remains famous for its annual Furry Dance and Hal-an-Tow ceremonies in May. Perhaps the largest change for the long term has been the closing down of Kerrier District Council and the emergence of "One Cornwall One Council" and the establishment of "Helston and the Lizard Community Network" with Helston at its centre.

One Cornwall One Council

The Local Government White Paper 'Strong and Prosperous Communities' was published by the Department of Communities and Local Government in October 2006.

Amongst other things, the white paper offered councils in two tier areas (where there were separate county and district councils) the opportunity to submit proposals to reorganise the local arrangements and set up new unitary councils.

The district was formed on 1 April 1974, as a merger of the borough of Helston, the urban district of Camborne-Redruth and Kerrier Rural District. On the 25 July 2007, Cornwall County Council's bid for unitary authority status was accepted by the government and next day the Western Morning News *printed the headline :*
"Local Councils will be scrapped, Cornwall wins bid to have Unitary status."

On 1 April 2009, Kerrier District Council was abolished and the new "Cornwall Council" came into being on the same day, with new elections being held on 4 June 2009.

Community Networks

Throughout Cornwall there are 19 community networks based around groupings of parishes and electoral divisions. Helston and the Lizard Community Network is one of these. Helston has one of the Council's "One Stop Shops" which brings advice and information on all council services closer to where people live, including housing, benefits, council tax, business rates, refuse and recycling and tourist information. Within the shop people can get help to fill in forms, hand in documents and speak to a council specialist either in person or by phone. Benefits and housing specialists visit a number of the One Stop Shops regularly, as do advisors from a range of non-council help organisations.

New houses on the site of the old Harvey's Yard.

New Buildings in Helston

Several new small estates have been built on brown field sites within the old town itself, for example the houses pictured above were built on the site of the old Harvey's Yard, off Godolphin Road in 2004, and the houses below were built on the garden of the old Kerrier District Offices at the "Willows" in Church Street.

Further small estates have been built on the former Graham's, the Builder's Merchants site and also in Shute Hill, on the site of the old Wesleyan Day School, a stylish development of nine one-bedroomed cottages within has taken place.

In addition to these new purpose-built buildings many conversions of existing properties have taken place. The largest of which was the conversion, in 2000, of the old Meneage Hospital by

Attractive town houses on the garden of the former Kerrier District Offices.

Penwith Housing development at Meneage House.

Penwith Housing.

Other conversions included the formation of 5 one bedroomed flats within the old Bible Christian Chapel in Meneage Street.

New By-pass

On 1 July 2005, a relief road from Gwealdues to Clodgey Way was opened, and in 2007 Helston Town Council supported a scheme for Taylor Wimpey Developments to build 191 homes on land between Clodgey Lane and the new relief road. In April 2008 Planning permission for a further 190 houses beyond the Bosnoweth Estate and north of the relief road was granted. This new development, known as Acres Edge, has proved to be very popular and offers a wide selection of 2, 3 and 4 bedroomed homes, many with garages, private gardens and allocated parking.

Public Buildings

In June 2003 Helston Fire Station moved from Trengrouse Way to Water-ma-trout. The old Fire Station initially became an Internet Café, but is now a "Mobility Centre". In May 2006 a New Helston Rugby Clubhouse and facilities were opened in Clodgey Lane and in Sept 2008 Whitbread opened a Travelodge on the southern side of the Relief Road together with a separate restaurant, called the Bay Tree.

Three New Super Markets

In December 2006 Plans were passed for the Lidl supermarket in St John's. This opened on 13 December 2007. In 2008 Flambards sought planning permission for a supermarket and petrol station, which was opened as Sainsburys. Not to be outdone, Tesco built a much larger store next to their existing store which, when the larger store was up and running they knocked down and turned into a much larger car-park.

These developments have caused concern, however, for the viability of the town centre. Although the Cornwall Retail Study (2010) concluded that the health of the town centre was considered to be good, several shops have since closed, including national retailers Dorothy Perkins and New Look, Wards the Florists, Eddy & Sons, Verran's Butchers, E.T.S., Woolworth, Carlyon's Newsagent, Perfect Shape Ladies Hairdresser, Brownbare Surfware Shop, and Togs Ladies Wear in Church Street. The Retail Study recommended that in future retail developers should focus on identifying proposals which can maintain and enhance the town centre.

Only 1 of the 24 shops in the 1985 advertisement existed in 2012.

Helston Railway Preservation Society

The original Helston Railway Preservation Society was formed on 18 May 2002. Four years later it became the Helston Railway Preservation Company Limited with the intent to build and run a railway, as a 'not for profit' company, limited by guarantee.

The objective of the company is to restore to running order, and re-open as a heritage railway, as much of the old Helston branch line as possible; the long term aim is to re-open a three mile section of the branch line between Nancegollan and Helston, Water-ma-Trout.

With the kind permission of the landowner, a volunteer labour force, drawn from the Company's supporters, started clearing the track bed at Trevarno Estate on Sunday 24 April 2005. Since that time the volunteers have worked wonders; starting with a totally overgrown, and in some places impenetrable track bed, the team has cleared and made ready just over a mile down to the formation. Over ¾ mile of new track has been laid, starting at Gansey in the north and travelling south through the Trevarno Estate down towards the original site of Truthall Halt. The new Trevarno Station has been constructed within the Trevarno Gardens and the Company has been granted planning permission to reinstate Truthall Halt.

Culdrose in the 21st Century

In the middle of May 2012, RNAS Culdrose played a major part in successfully bringing the Olympic Flame to Land's End for the start of the Olympic Torch Relay around the whole of the United Kingdom.

Although over the years the emphasis has changed from fixed wing fighter aircraft to rotary Culdrose remains Britain's largest military helicopter operating base and is home to many Fleet Air Arm Units operating a variety of aircraft types. At present there are two main types of helicopter at Culdrose, the Sea King and the Merlin.

The Airborne Surveillance and Control (ASaC) squadrons, 849, 854 and 857 Naval Air Squadrons, all equipped with the Mk VII Sea King, provide an "eye-in-the-sky" capability giving vital information to command at sea or on land. Originally designed to identify potential aerial targets and provide early warning to the Fleet at sea, the Searchwater 2000 radar and system operators in the ASaC helicopters have proved highly effective at tracking both maritime and land targets over a wide area and in many different environments, most notably during current operations in Afghanistan.

771 Naval Air Squadron operates the HAR5 version in the Search & Rescue (SAR) role. These red and grey coloured helicopters are on call 24 hours a day 365 days a year providing coverage over a 250 mile radius from Culdrose. Apart from two pilots (equipped with night vision goggles for difficult missions in the dark) each Sea King is crewed by an observer and an aircrewman, who is also trained in first aid. The Squadron has been called upon to perform a myriad of rescue missions: sailors in distress, downed aircrew (thankfully very rarely), flood victims, missing or injured climbers, tourists who've fallen down cliffs, people involved in road accidents, and medical emergencies. They perform hundreds of missions each year and save countless lives.

The crew from 771 Naval Air Squadron who flew the Sea King helicopter with the Olympic Flame from Culdrose to Land's End.

820 Naval Air Squadron, one of the Navy's trio of front-line Merlin helicopter squadrons, takes it in turns with its sister squadron 814, also based at Culdrose, to support the international effort against illegal activities on the high seas east of Suez – piracy, people-trafficking, smuggling, drug-running and terrorism.

829 Naval Air Squadron – "the Kingfishers" – provides the Navy's Type 23 frigates with the Merlin helicopters they need to operate around the world. The squadron provides dedicated Merlin 'flights' – that's one helicopter, a full complement of aircrew (two pilots, one observer, and one aircrewman) and a nine-strong maintenance team – for the Navy's Type 23 frigate fleet, wherever they're operating in the world.

Fixed wing assets at Culdrose include the Jetstream T2s of 750 NAS which is responsible for training observers for the front line units, training which includes navigation, radio and radar techniques and tactical skills.

The Fleet Requirements Air Direction Unit (FRADU) Hawks provide the high speed tasks for the Royal Navy. These aircraft are still owned by the RAF and are only leased by the Navy, being operated by Hunting Aviation and flown and maintained by civilians.

The Cattle Market and Coronation Park

The last Cattle Market was held on 21 February 2001, its demise as a consequence of the widespread Foot and Mouth disease that devastated the farming community. During the next four years major plans for the development of the area came into fruition. The official opening of Phase One of the improvement scheme took place in December 2006 with great outdoor leisure facilities and a larger 21st century restaurant. The "Fat Stock Show" was last held in the cattle market in October 2005, but it continued in an excellent facility at Franchive Farm on the Redruth Road, by courtesy of Mr Bob Cowell.

The new "Old Cattle Market" building.

The Re-development of Helston Cattle Market

During the third week of April 2011 a significant milestone for the town of Helston was achieved when construction work began on the site of the Old Cattle Market. The project, which is managed by South Kerrier Alliance Community Interest Company (SKA) reached this stage only after many months of hard work by the SKA team in raising £1.875M of funds from Local, Regional, National and European sources. Cornwall Council has also supported the project. (South Kerrier Alliance Community Interest Company is a social enterprise, formed by volunteers, to address the needs and aspirations of the people of South Kerrier, Helston and its surrounding parishes).

Construction of the new building commenced in mid May 2011 with the opening of the new centre at the end of March 2012. The Old Cattle Market has dedicated space on the first floor for business units and at present has been leased to a local finance company, a local business woman selling environmentally friendly baby items, the Lizard Trust, an autism charity and a solicitor, who incidentally used to visit the building as a child with his grandfather to sell cattle. The west wing on the ground floor hosts another wonderful tenant, Cornwall Council's Adult Care and Support Team allowing carers to drop their charges off in Helston a much closer destination to their homes. In addition the modern spacious community hall is an open plan space which is catering for a wide variety of events. This area is already being used by small to large community groups, commercial events, business training, live events and weddings – this new community centric building caters for every local need and is helping to regenerate the area.

Helston Schools

During the past decade the Governance of Schools has changed, the Local Education Authorities have been disbanded and more and more schools across the country are working with a much wider range of partners such as businesses, universities, charities, the voluntary sector and other schools as a possible way of raising standards. By harnessing the expertise of these partners, schools can offer a wider range of opportunities, helping to raise attainment and ensuring that every child has a chance to increase their potential.

As from 31 December 2011 seventeen schools in the Helston Area have chosen to continue to be part of the local authority, but will now also be supported by, "The Helston and Lizard Peninsula Educational Partnership Trust", a Charitable Trust with partners drawn from the University of Cornwall, Cornwall County Council, Truro Diocesan Board of Education etc.

Schools, supported by the Trust, plan to work together to promote aspiration, encourage ambition and ensure achievement. The Trust will also develop services to support schools, young people and their families in our local communities.

Helston Receives the Olympic Torch

On Friday 18 May 2012 the Olympic Torch arrived at RNAS Culdrose, before starting its 70 day tour across the UK the following day.

At 10.20 am on 19 May, at the welcome to Helston sign on the Penzance Road, the Olympic Torch, which had started its day at Lands End, started its relay through Helston, by way of St John's with its new "Old Market" community building, up past the Gryll's Memorial arch and into a packed Coinagehall Street, just like Flora Day all over again, past the Town Hall into Wendron Street and on into Godolphin Road, ending at Falmouth Road just 18 minutes later.

Crowds of people packing Coinagehall Street to view the passage of the Olympic Torch through Helston.